RELATIONSHIP DEVOTIONAL FOR COUPLES:

SIMPLE DAILY REFLECTIONS TO BUILD FAITH, DEEPEN COMMUNICATION, REKINDLE LOVE, AND STRENGTHEN YOUR BOND EVEN ON BUSY DAYS

DEAN RAMSEY

CONTENTS

Introduction:The Couples Devotional workbook for a better relationship   v

1. Building a Foundation of Faith   1
2. Enhancing Communication Daily   12
3. Embracing Diversity in Faith and Practice   24
4. Integrating Devotion into Daily Life   33
   Review   43
5. Navigating Life Transitions Together   45
6. Financial Harmony and Planning   55
7. Balancing Individual and Shared Goals   65
8. Creating a Positive and Supportive Environment   78
9. Sustaining Long-term Relationship Health   88
10. Overcoming Objections and Challenges   97
11. 52 unique daily reflections   106
12. Daily Reflections   110
13. The Transformative Power of Daily Reflections and
    Devotions   118

   Review   131
   Conclusion   133
   Bibliography   137

INTRODUCTION: THE COUPLES DEVOTIONAL WORKBOOK FOR A BETTER RELATIONSHIP

My passion for helping couples like you comes from years of experience and dedication. I've seen firsthand how communication barriers can create distance, and I've worked tirelessly to find ways to bridge that gap. It's my mission to guide you toward a more meaningful connection.

Through customer insights, we learned that couples like you want relatable content and practical exercises. You want advice that feels genuine and let me tell you about John and Lisa. They had been married for ten years, but lately, they felt more like roommates than partners. Their days were packed with work, kids, and chores. It seemed they barely had time to say "hello," let alone connect on a deeper level. One day, a friend told them about daily devotionals for couples. Skeptical but hopeful, they decided to give it a try. Each morning, they spent just a few minutes reading and reflecting together. Slowly, they began to notice a change. Their communication improved, their love rekindled, and their bond grew stronger. Those precious moments became the anchor in their busy lives.

Stories like theirs inspire this book. It aims to provide you and your partner practical and spiritual tools to strengthen your bond through daily reflections and devotionals. Whether you are newlyweds or have been together for decades, these tools aim to bring you closer and deepen your connection.

We approach this book with a unique vision. We've combined proven strategies, meaningful Bible verses, and a daily devotion plan. This ensures you receive fresh, impactful content that avoids repetition and keeps you engaged. The aim is to offer something new daily to help you grow together in faith and love.

I know life is busy. It often feels like there should be more hours in the day to focus on your relationship. But this book is written for you because you desire a deeper connection and faith integration. It's designed to fit into your life, not add to the stress. A few minutes a day can transform how you relate to each other.

Not overly prescriptive, We've listened to and crafted content that speaks to your experiences and offers real solutions.

What sets this book apart is its dynamic structure. You will find multimedia integration and personalized paths for your journey, making it adaptable to your unique needs as a couple. Some days, you might enjoy a video reflection, while other days, a written devotional or a simple exercise might be just what you need.

I promise that engaging with this book, you will find ways to build faith, deepen communication, rekindle love, and strengthen your bond. Even in your busiest times, these daily reflections will be your sanctuary of connection.

I encourage you to commit to this journey of daily devotionals. Expect transformation and growth. It's a shared adventure that promises to enrich your relationship and spiritual life.

As you embark on this path, know that the book's roadmap is designed to be transformative. Together, you will explore faith, communication, love, and bonding. As you turn each page, you'll find yourselves eager for the next step in this spiritual and relational adventure. Let's begin this journey together.

CHAPTER 1

BUILDING A FOUNDATION
OF FAITH

S arah and Mike had always considered themselves a close
couple. However, their connection started to fray when life
threw them a few curveballs. Between career changes,
moving to a new city, and caring for an aging parent, they felt the
world's weight pressing on them. One evening, after a particularly
challenging day, they decided to try something new that could
anchor them amidst the chaos. They began incorporating daily
devotionals into their routine. It was a simple commitment but
soon became the steady force that helped them navigate life's
unpredictability with grace and unity. Their story is not unique;
many couples find that faith guides them safely back to each other
like a lighthouse in a storm.

The Spiritual Core: Establishing Faith Together

In relationships, faith acts as a stabilizing force, offering support
and guidance when uncertainty looms. The Bible speaks to this
foundational role, emphasizing faith's power to sustain love and
commitment. For example, 1 Corinthians 13:4-7 describes love as
patient and kind, underscoring the faith-driven virtues that

strengthen bonds. Similarly, Ephesians 5:21-33 advocates for mutual love and respect, principles that faith instills in couples seeking enduring connection. Many couples credit their lasting relationships to the faith they share, which provides a moral and spiritual framework that helps them navigate challenges with resilience and hope. When you let faith into your relationship, it becomes a source of strength and stability, guiding you toward a deeper, more meaningful connection.

To build this foundation, it's essential to identify and articulate your shared spiritual values. Consider what matters most to you in your faith journey, and explore these values together. Creating a worksheet that distinguishes your shared values from individual beliefs is helpful. This exercise encourages open dialogue and collaboration, allowing you to understand each other's spiritual perspectives more fully. Use discussion prompts to facilitate these conversations, asking questions like, "What role does faith play in our relationship?" or "How can we support each other's spiritual growth?" As you explore these questions, you'll uncover shared values that serve as the bedrock of your relationship.

Cultivating daily spiritual practices can further enhance your connection. Start with simple routines that integrate spirituality into your everyday life. Morning prayer routines can set a positive tone for the day, allowing you to center yourselves and align your intentions. In the evening, gratitude journals provide an opportunity to reflect on the day's blessings and express appreciation for one another. These practices don't have to be lengthy or complicated; even a few minutes spent together in quiet reflection can foster a sense of peace and unity.

Establishing mutual spiritual goals can also strengthen your bond. Discuss what you hope to achieve together in your spiritual journey, setting attainable goals you can work towards as a couple. For instance, aim to read a spiritual book together within a month or volunteer at a local charity regularly. Long-term goals could involve participating in a spiritual retreat or committing to a regular service in your community. These goals deepen your spiritual connection and provide shared experiences that build trust and intimacy.

Faith in a relationship is a source of strength and a catalyst for growth. By establishing a spiritual core together, you can navigate life's challenges with greater confidence and resilience, knowing you have a solid foundation to support you both. This chapter aims to guide you in building that foundation, offering insights and practical tools to help you strengthen your bond through faith.

Sacred Space: Creating an Inviting Environment for Devotion

Imagine your home as a canvas, waiting to become a sanctuary of peace and reflection. In the hustle and bustle of everyday life, having a sacred space dedicated to spiritual practice can be a refuge. It's more than just a physical location; it's a mindset. This space acts as a psychological anchor, grounding you amidst chaos. It's where you and your partner can retreat from the world, find solace, and connect on a deeper level. Studies show that having a dedicated area for spiritual activities can enhance focus and foster a sense of calm, making it easier to maintain regular devotionals. It's like having a personal oasis, a place where you can leave your worries at the door and enter with an open mind and heart.

Creating this space involves more than just picking a spot in your home. It's about designing an environment that invites reflection and connection. Begin by choosing a location that feels right for both of you. It could be a quiet corner in your living room, a cozy nook in your bedroom, or even a garden spot where nature enhances the serenity. Pay attention to the ambiance—soft lighting, soothing colors, and comfortable seating can make a world of difference. Incorporate meaningful symbols and artifacts that resonate with your spiritual journey. Perhaps a family Bible, a candle, or a small statue that holds sentimental value. These items become touchstones, reminding you of your commitment to each other and spiritual growth.

Maintaining the sacredness of this space is crucial. Establish ground rules to ensure it remains special and undisturbed. It could be a no-tech zone where only spiritual and positive conversations happen. Consider setting specific times when the space is used for devotionals to reinforce its purpose. This consistency creates a ritual, transforming the space into a sacred haven that nurtures your relationship.

In today's digital age, technology can be a double-edged sword. While it offers incredible resources, it can also distract from the sacredness you're trying to cultivate. Mindful integration is key. Use technology to enhance, not detract. Apps for guided meditations or spiritual readings can complement your practices without intruding. Choose tech that supports your goals, like audio devotionals or ambient soundscapes that promote relaxation. Using technology thoughtfully enriches your spiritual experience without compromising the sanctity of your sacred space.

Integrating Scripture into Daily Life

Imagine waking up to the gentle glow of morning light, the world still quiet, offering a perfect moment to connect with scripture. This can be your daily reality, a time when you and your partner anchor yourselves in spiritual wisdom. By incorporating morning scripture devotionals into your routine, you set a powerful tone for the day. Choose verses that speak to both of you, focusing on love, patience, or guidance themes. As you read and reflect together, you'll find these moments create a shared sense of peace and purpose. Scripture-based affirmations can further enrich this practice. By starting the day with affirming words drawn from sacred texts, you cultivate a mindset of positivity and strength. These affirmations remind you of your shared values, reinforcing a united front as you face the day's challenges together.

Scripture serves as an invaluable guide, especially when navigating relationship hurdles. During conflicts, turning to scripture can provide clarity and direction. It encourages a more compassionate approach, helping you see beyond immediate frustrations. For instance, verses on forgiveness and understanding can diffuse tension, allowing for calm and constructive dialogue. Scripture becomes a compass, steering your decisions with wisdom and grace. When faced with tough choices, let these sacred words inform your path. They offer insights that transcend personal biases, grounding your decisions in love and integrity.

Beyond guidance, scripture inspires and motivates, breathing new life into your relationship. Regularly explore verses that celebrate love and commitment, allowing them to invigorate your bond. Select passages that resonate with your relationship's unique rhythm, using them as reminders of your shared journey. These scriptures can act as touchstones, sparking conversations about your hopes and dreams. They remind you of the beauty in your partnership, encouraging you to cherish and nurture it.

To weave scripture seamlessly into your lives:

1. Develop a habit of sharing insights with one another.
2. Create a daily ritual where you discuss meaningful passages, perhaps over breakfast or during a quiet evening walk.
3. Share your interpretations and listen to each other's perspectives.

This exchange deepens your understanding, fostering a richer connection to scripture and each other. It becomes a dance of dialogue, where you learn and grow together, guided by the wisdom of sacred texts.

Interactive Element: Daily Scripture Sharing Exercise

Objective: Deepen your connection by sharing and discussing scripture daily.

Instructions:

1. **Select a Verse**: Choose a verse that resonates with you each morning. It could be something that speaks to a current situation or a passage that uplifts your spirit.
2. **Reflect Individually**: Spend a few moments contemplating the verse. Consider what it means to you personally and how it applies to your relationship.
3. **Share Together**: Set aside time in the evening to share your reflections. Discuss what the verse means to each of you and any insights it inspired.
4. **Listen Actively**: As your partner shares, listen without interruption. Offer encouragement and ask questions to deepen the discussion.
5. **Apply the Insights**: Consider how you might apply the verse's teachings in your daily lives. Identify a small action you can take as a couple to embody its message.

Engaging in this exercise regularly can transform how you perceive and interact with scripture, making it an integral part of your relationship's foundation.

Faith Journey Mapping: Understanding Each Other's Spiritual Paths

Imagine sitting side by side with your partner, tracing the intricate path of your spiritual pasts, like explorers charting familiar yet individual territories. This exercise encourages you to delve into each other's spiritual histories, ensuring a richer understanding of where each of you stands today. It's not about finding differences but discovering the influences that have shaped each other. Consider creating a spiritual life timeline, a visual representation of significant moments that have impacted your faith. Maybe it's the memory of a childhood church, a conversation with a wise mentor, or a time when you felt a spiritual epiphany. These experiences form the tapestry of your faith, and sharing them openly can lead to a profound appreciation for the unique journeys that have brought you to this point.

Facilitating open sharing is crucial for this process. It's about creating a safe space where you can share without fear of judgment or comparison. Start with dialogue prompts that gently guide the conversation. Ask questions like, "What was a pivotal moment in your spiritual life?" or "How has your faith evolved over the years?" As you listen, practice empathy and curiosity, allowing your partner's stories to unfold without interruption. This isn't about whose path is "better" or more "correct." Instead, it's an opportunity to see the world through your partner's eyes, to understand the depth of their spiritual identity, and to celebrate the diversity of experiences that enrich your relationship.

As you share, you may notice areas where your spiritual paths intersect. These intersections are the places where your beliefs and values align, providing fertile ground for connection. Engage in exercises to identify these complementary beliefs. Discuss how your individual values and experiences can complement one another, building a stronger bond. For instance, you both value compassion, manifesting it in different ways. One might volunteer at a local shelter, while the other donate to causes they care deeply about. Recognizing these overlaps allows you to strengthen your partnership, drawing on shared values as a source of unity and strength.

With this newfound understanding, create a joint faith map. This visual representation can be as simple or elaborate as you like. Use it to chart your shared spiritual journey, highlighting future aspirations. Include milestones you wish to achieve together, like attending a spiritual retreat or starting a new tradition. This map becomes a living document, a testament to your evolving spiritual connection. It serves as a guide for your relationship and a reminder of the shared faith that binds you. Pull out your map during challenging times to remind yourselves of the goals you've set and the growth you've achieved together.

In this process, remember that patience and openness are your allies. The goal is to deepen your understanding of each other, fostering a more harmonious and resilient relationship grounded in mutual respect and love. As you embark on this exploration, you will find that mapping your spiritual paths enriches your bond and enhances your personal faith, creating a tapestry of shared experiences and aspirations that strengthen your connection.

Integrating Diverse Beliefs: Finding Common Ground

In the tapestry of life, no two threads are the same, yet they can weave together to create something beautiful. This is especially true for couples with diverse beliefs. Embracing these differences can enrich a relationship but requires respect and understanding. Imagine a couple where one partner finds solace in quiet meditation while the other draws strength from vibrant church services. Both practices hold immense value, and acknowledging these differences is the first step toward harmony. Take inspiration from couples who have successfully harmonized their diverse beliefs. They often speak of respect as the key, a commitment to honor each other's practices without judgment. Such respect fosters an environment where both partners feel valued and understood, creating a foundation for deeper connection.

Finding common spiritual themes amidst differing beliefs is like discovering hidden treasures. It involves looking beyond the surface to the core values you share. These include compassion, integrity, or a commitment to service. Visualize these as overlapping circles in a Venn diagram. Each partner brings unique beliefs to the table, but it's the shared space that holds the potential for unity. Engaging in this exercise can uncover insights that strengthen your bond. As you explore, you may find that while your individual practices differ, the underlying principles align. This discovery can be enlightening and comforting, a reminder that you are on the same path despite your differences.

Developing interfaith practices and celebrating both traditions is another way to honor your unique spiritual identities. Consider crafting prayers incorporating elements from each faith, creating a ritual that feels inclusive and meaningful for both partners. Celebrating diverse holidays can also be a joyful expression of your shared life. Imagine planning festivities incorporating traditions from both backgrounds—a Christmas tree adorned with symbols from Diwali or a Passover meal that includes an Easter egg hunt. These practices honor your individual backgrounds and create new traditions unique to your relationship, making every celebration a testament to your unity.

Continuous learning about each other's faiths is crucial in promoting empathy and understanding. It's a lifelong endeavor that enriches your relationship and deepens your connection. Dive into books and resources that offer insights into each other's beliefs. This exploration can be enlightening, offering new perspectives and fostering a deeper appreciation for each other's spiritual journeys. Consider reading together or discussing what you've learned over a meal. This shared learning experience can spark meaningful conversations, allowing you to grow together in knowledge and understanding.

In this chapter, we focus on the beauty of diversity within relationships. By respecting differences, identifying common themes, and developing inclusive practices, couples can find a harmonious balance that honors both partners' beliefs. It's about creating a shared space where both can thrive, contributing to a resilient and nurturing relationship. This approach strengthens your bond and enriches your spiritual lives, paving the way for a deeper, more meaningful connection.

Covenant Commitment: Building a Strong Spiritual Bond

The concept of covenant in relationships speaks to a promise, a sacred bond that transcends mere agreement. In biblical terms, a covenant is more than a contract; it's a profound commitment that involves faith, trust, and love. This idea finds its roots in scriptures like Genesis 2:24, which talks about two becoming one, and Ephesians 5:31-33, which emphasizes unity and love in marriage. These passages highlight the depth and sanctity of commitment, encouraging couples to see their relationship as a sacred covenant before God. This covenant provides strength and stability, acting as a spiritual anchor that grounds the relationship through life's inevitable ups and downs.

Crafting a shared covenant vision can be a transformative experience. It invites you to reflect on the unique spiritual bond you share. Consider it a workshop of sorts, where you and your partner sit down to articulate your shared dreams, values, and commitments. Begin by discussing what a covenant means to each of you and how it can enhance your relationship. Write down your thoughts, aspirations, and promises to each other. This process can be deeply revealing, offering insights into your partnership that might surprise and delight you. The result is a personalized covenant that reflects your unique journey together, serving as a guide and a testament to your shared love and faith.

Rituals play a crucial role in reinforcing this covenant. They regularly remind you of your commitment, keeping it alive and vibrant. Consider creating anniversary covenant renewal ceremonies where you revisit and reaffirm your promises to one another. These can be simple or elaborate, depending on what resonates with you. Monthly covenant reflection sessions can also be beneficial. Set aside time to discuss how you're living out your covenant, what challenges you've faced, and how you've grown together. These rituals help keep your covenant at the forefront of your relationship, ensuring it remains a living, breathing part of your daily life.

Celebrating milestones within your covenant journey is equally important. These moments are opportunities to acknowledge and honor the growth and achievements you've experienced together. Think about ways to mark these occasions, whether it's a special dinner, a weekend getaway, or a simple but meaningful gesture. These celebrations don't have to be grand; what matters is the recognition of the hard work and dedication you both invest in your relationship. By acknowledging these milestones, you reinforce the strength of your covenant and the love that binds you.

As you continue to nurture your covenant, remember that it is a dynamic entity evolving alongside your relationship. It's a testament to your shared commitment, a source of inspiration and guidance. This covenant is a promise to each other and a foundation upon which you build a life of love, faith, and unity. Embrace this sacred bond, and let it guide you through the challenges and joys that lie ahead.

CHAPTER 2
ENHANCING COMMUNICATION DAILY

Think about the last time you and your partner had a conversation where you truly felt heard. It might have been over a cup of coffee or during a quiet walk. These moments, though simple, carry the power to transform relationships. They are built on the foundation of mindful listening. This skill goes beyond hearing words to genuinely understanding and connecting with your partner's thoughts and emotions. In our fast-paced world, it's easy to overlook this crucial aspect of communication, yet its impact is monumental. By practicing mindful listening, you open the door to deeper intimacy, greater empathy, and a bond that withstands the test of time.

Mindful listening is about being fully present. It means setting aside distractions and focusing entirely on your partner. It's a way of saying, "I value what you have to say." In relationships, this practice enhances intimacy and understanding, as noted by the Institute for Family Studies, which emphasizes that mindful listening fosters trust and reduces conflict. The benefits are profound—improved communication, increased empathy, and a stronger emotional connection, to name a few. When you listen mindfully, you validate your partner's feelings and experiences, creating a safe space for open dialogue.

There are several techniques you can employ to become an active listener. Start with the "Reflect and Clarify" method. As your partner speaks, reflect on what you've heard to ensure understanding. This might sound like, "So what I'm hearing is..." or "Let me make sure I got that right..." This technique confirms comprehension and shows your partner that you are engaged. Non-verbal cues also play a significant role. Nodding, maintaining eye contact, and offering gestures of empathy can communicate understanding without words. These subtle signals reinforce that you are present and invested in the conversation.

Obstacles to active listening are common but are manageable. Distractions, both internal and external, can disrupt focus. Make it a point to set aside phones, turn off the TV, and find a quiet space where you can genuinely connect. Emotional triggers can also hinder listening. If you feel defensive or agitated, take a moment to breathe and center yourself before responding. Acknowledging these barriers is the first step toward overcoming them, paving the way for more meaningful interactions.

Consider incorporating weekly listening sessions into your routine to hone your listening skills. These can be informal, over dinner, or during a leisurely walk. The goal is to create a dedicated time where listening is prioritized. Practice the techniques discussed during these sessions, and reflect on what you've learned. Over time, this practice will become second nature, enriching your connection and enhancing your communication.

Interactive Element: Weekly Listening Session Guide

Objective: Strengthen communication by practicing active listening techniques.

Instructions:

1. **Schedule a Time**: Choose a day and time each week for a dedicated listening session. Make it a priority, just like any other important meeting.
2. **Create a Comfortable Environment**: Find a quiet space where you both feel relaxed and free from distractions. Consider lighting a candle or playing soft background music to set the mood.
3. **Practice Reflect and Clarify**: As one partner speaks, the other should reflect back what they hear, using phrases like "It sounds like you're saying..." or "What I understand is..." This ensures clarity and understanding.
4. **Incorporate Non-Verbal Cues**: Use eye contact, nods, and empathetic gestures to show engagement and support.
5. **Discuss and Reflect**: At the end of the session, discuss how the process felt. What worked well? What could be improved? Use this reflection to enhance future sessions.

Heart Check: Opening Emotional Doors

Imagine having a space where you and your partner can regularly open up, explore feelings, and connect deeply. This is the essence of a heart check. It's a scheduled time dedicated to discussing emotional well-being, a practice that maintains the health of your relationship. Heart checks act as a preventative measure, helping you address issues before they escalate. These discussions are not about fixing problems on the spot but about creating a consistent habit of checking in with each other. This method fosters an environment where emotional intimacy can thrive, ensuring both partners feel heard and understood.

Establishing a regular schedule is key to conducting an effective heart check. Consistency is crucial. Choose a time that suits both of you, perhaps once a week or every other week. The goal is to make it a routine, something you both look forward to. Creating an open and honest dialogue environment is equally important. Approach these sessions with empathy and patience, ensuring both partners feel safe sharing without judgment. Start by setting the tone with simple gestures like turning off phones or lighting a candle—anything that signals this is a special, dedicated time.

You can use specific questions to guide the conversation during your heart checks. For instance, asking, "What has been on your mind lately?" opens the floor for discussing current thoughts and emotions. It's an invitation for your partner to share anything that might be weighing on them. Another effective question is, "How can I support you better?" This shows a willingness to adapt and grow together, emphasizing your commitment to being there for each other. These questions encourage reflection and honesty, deepening the connection between you.

Regular heart checks have a profound impact on your relationship. They help prevent emotional disconnect by keeping lines of communication open. Over time, they build a habit of vulnerability, where sharing feelings becomes second nature. This practice enhances trust and emotional intimacy, creating a foundation where both partners feel secure and supported. As you continue with these heart checks, you'll likely find that your relationship becomes more resilient and able to weather challenges with grace and understanding.

Navigating Busy Schedules

In today's world, balancing work, family, and personal time can feel like juggling flaming torches. It's no wonder communication sometimes takes a back seat. With demanding jobs and endless to-do lists, carving out time for meaningful conversations might seem daunting. Often, the imbalance between work and life leads to emotional disconnect. You may find yourself so caught up in the hustle that you and your partner drift apart without even realizing it. It's like living parallel lives under the same roof, where the days blur into weeks, and suddenly, you can't remember the last time you really talked.

So, how do you make communication a priority amidst the chaos? First, consider setting daily check-in times. It doesn't have to be anything elaborate—a quick chat over breakfast or a text during lunch can work wonders. Technology can be your ally here. Use video calls or voice notes to maintain that connection even when you're miles apart. It's about finding those pockets of time that can be transformed into moments of connection. Remember, quality trumps quantity. A ten-minute conversation where you're both fully present is worth more than an hour of distracted chatter. Focused, uninterrupted time allows you to engage with each other, making every word count truly.

Integrating communication into your daily routine doesn't have to be a chore. Get creative with it. If you commute together, use that time for "commute conversations." Discuss your plans for the day, share something funny, or simply enjoy each other's company. If mornings are your thing, why not have "morning coffee catch-ups"? Take those few minutes before the day takes over to connect and align. It's about making the most of your time, turning ordinary moments into opportunities for connection. This way, even the busiest schedules can become fertile ground for meaningful interactions, allowing your relationship to flourish despite the chaos of daily life.

Prayer Partnering: Strengthening Communication through Prayer

Imagine starting your day with a moment of shared stillness, hands intertwined, voices united in prayer. The act of praying together can be a powerful way to enhance communication and spiritual intimacy in your relationship. Couples who engage in this practice often find that it creates a deeper connection, reinforcing their bond and providing a shared sense of purpose. Case studies highlight how prayer can transform relationships, offering couples a sacred space to express gratitude, seek guidance, and find peace. This shared spiritual practice can open new doors, fostering empathy and understanding that transcends words.

Developing a consistent prayer routine is easier than you think. Begin with morning prayer sessions that set a positive tone for the day. These moments can be as simple as expressing gratitude for each other or asking for strength to face the challenges ahead. Evening reflections offer an opportunity to unwind together, providing a space to reflect on the day's events and seek guidance for the future. Establishing these routines can create a comforting rhythm in your lives, anchoring your relationship in faith and love. As you grow accustomed to these practices, you'll find that prayer becomes a natural and cherished part of your daily interactions.

Bringing personal and relational concerns into your prayer life can deepen your connection. Creating a shared prayer list is a practical way to address these concerns collectively. Take time to discuss what's on your mind, whether it's a work challenge, a family issue, or a shared goal. Pray over these topics, inviting divine wisdom into your relationship. This practice strengthens your spiritual bond and encourages open communication as you share your worries and hopes with each other and a higher power. It becomes a collaborative effort, a joint commitment to supporting each other through faith.

Prayer can also serve as a powerful tool for conflict resolution. When tensions rise, turning to prayer can offer a different perspective, shifting the focus from immediate frustration to a broader understanding. Meditative prayer sessions allow you to pause and reflect, fostering patience and compassion. Forgiveness prayers can help release resentment, paving the way for reconciliation and healing. In these moments, prayer acts as a bridge, connecting you to each other and to a source of wisdom that guides you toward resolution and peace.

Communicating Through Life Transitions

Life has a way of throwing curveballs when you least expect them. Whether moving to a new city, starting a new career, or welcoming a baby, these transitions can test even the strongest relationships. During these times, communication becomes your lifeline. Anticipating the need for open dialogue can prevent misunderstandings and build resilience. Engage in anticipation exercises by discussing potential changes and their impacts before they happen. This proactive approach allows you to prepare emotionally and logistically, reducing the shock of sudden shifts. By acknowledging the challenges that come with life transitions, you can navigate them with clarity and unity.

Regular check-ins become crucial during periods of change. Set up a schedule that suits you both, perhaps weekly, to discuss how you're feeling and address concerns. These discussions should be safe spaces where honesty reigns. Craft transition-specific communication plans tailored to your unique situation. They might include special times for discussion or even written notes if verbal communication feels too intense. Flexibility is key. Adapting your communication style to fit new circumstances can ease the transition. If emotions run high, embrace adaptive techniques like switching from face-to-face talks to written notes. This adaptability fosters understanding and maintains harmony.

Supporting each other emotionally through these times is vital. Offer validation by acknowledging your partner's experiences and feelings. It's easy to get caught up in your emotions and forget that your partner is also experiencing the transition. Use emotional support strategies like active listening and empathy to ensure your partner feels heard and valued. This mutual support creates a foundation of trust and love that can weather any storm. Remember, it's not just about surviving these changes but thriving together. Embrace the journey, knowing that every challenge faced together strengthens your bond.

Gratitude Journaling: Sharing Daily Blessings

Gratitude is like a glue that binds us closer, strengthening emotional bonds in ways we might not even realize. Research shows that expressing gratitude can boost relationship satisfaction, making both partners feel more appreciated and valued. Focusing on the positive aspects of your life and relationship creates a ripple effect of happiness and contentment. You begin to notice the little things that often go unnoticed, and this awareness can transform how you relate to each other. It's like seeing your partner through a lens of appreciation, highlighting their efforts and love in new ways. This appreciation fosters a deeper connection, reinforcing the emotional ties that keep you together.

Starting a shared gratitude journal can be a simple yet profound way to capture these moments. Begin by choosing a journal that you both like. It doesn't have to be fancy; even a notebook will do. Set aside a few minutes daily to write down what you're grateful for. You could jot down three things you appreciated about your partner that day. Swap turns or write together—whatever feels right. The key is consistency. This practice documents the blessings in your lives and provides a tangible reminder of the love and joy you share.

Incorporating daily gratitude rituals into your routine is another way to keep gratitude alive in your relationship. You might start each morning by sharing one thing you're thankful for over breakfast. It sets a positive tone for the day, reminding you of the good in your lives. In the evening, reflect on the day's positive moments. What made you smile? What small act of kindness did you appreciate? These reflections can be shared during dinner or before bed, creating a nightly ritual focusing on gratitude and connection.

Periodically reviewing your journal entries can be a wonderful way to reinforce your shared appreciation. Set aside time each month to look back at what you've written. Discuss the entries that stand out, and share how they made you feel. This review strengthens your bond and keeps gratitude fresh in your mind. It's a chance to celebrate the love you have and the journey you're on, fostering a deeper appreciation for each other and the life you're building together.

Intimacy Reboot: Strategies for Emotional Closeness

Let's talk about emotional intimacy. That warm feeling of closeness and understanding makes your relationship feel special. But sometimes, past experiences can overshadow how you connect today. There may have been moments when the vulnerability was met with misunderstanding, or past relationships left scars. These memories can create barriers, making it difficult to open up and truly connect. It's important to recognize these factors. They can quietly undermine closeness, keeping you at arm's length when you only want to be closer. Understanding these barriers is the first step in addressing them. By acknowledging what holds you back, you can begin to dismantle those walls and pave the way for genuine connection.

Creating emotional safety is key to rebuilding intimacy. This means crafting a space where both of you feel comfortable sharing your innermost thoughts and feelings. Start by setting clear boundaries and expectations for how you communicate. You may agree to always listen without interrupting or perhaps avoid specific phrases that trigger defensiveness. These small agreements can make a big difference, providing a framework that encourages openness. When both partners feel secure, expressing vulnerability and exploring deeper emotional connections becomes easier without fear of judgment or rejection.

Mindfulness practices can also play a crucial role in enhancing emotional connection. By being present and attentive, you can cultivate empathy and understanding. Consider guided meditation for couples as a practical tool. It encourages both of you to focus on the moment, tuning into each other's emotions and needs. This shared experience can deepen your bond, creating a sense of unity and appreciation. Practicing mindfulness together enhances your connection and fosters a sense of peace and relaxation, allowing intimacy to flourish naturally.

To rekindle emotional closeness, engage in meaningful activities that bring you together. "Remember When" storytelling evenings can be a delightful way to stroll down memory lane. Share stories from your past, recalling moments that made you laugh, cry, or feel particularly close. These stories remind you of the history you've built together, reinforcing your bond. Conversations about shared goals and dreams can also reignite intimacy. Discussing your future aspirations—whether traveling the world or building a family—can create a shared vision that strengthens your connection. These conversations foster a sense of partnership, reminding you that you're not just individuals but a team united by love and shared dreams.

Expressing Needs with Love and Respect

Clearly, identifying what you need is crucial to feeling understood and valued in any relationship. It's not just about knowing what you want but being able to express it in a way that's clear and respectful. Imagine creating a 'needs list'—a simple yet powerful tool where you jot down what matters to you, from emotional support to daily routines. By articulating your needs this way, you give yourself and your partner a roadmap to understanding each other better. This clarity prevents misunderstandings and helps avoid the resentment that can build when needs are left unspoken.

Using 'I' statements can transform how you communicate these needs. Instead of saying, "You never listen to me," try, "I feel unheard when we talk, and it's important for me to feel connected." This subtle shift from 'you' to 'I' avoids casting blame and opens the door for constructive conversation. It's about owning your feelings and needs without making your partner feel attacked. Practicing this approach can lead to more productive and loving discussions where both partners feel safe to share.

Balancing assertiveness with compassion is key. You want to state your needs confidently while remaining sensitive to your partner's feelings. Consider assertiveness exercises where you practice stating your needs in a calm and straightforward manner. Pair this with compassionate dialogue practices, like acknowledging your partner's perspective before expressing your own. This balance ensures that both of you feel heard and respected, setting the stage for mutual understanding and growth.

Handling rejection and negotiation is part of expressing needs. Only some requests will be met with agreement, and that's okay. Prepare for these moments with negotiation role-plays. These exercises help you explore solutions that work for both of you. Develop coping strategies for unmet needs, focusing on understanding the reasons behind them and finding common ground. This approach fosters resilience and adaptability, allowing you to navigate relationship dynamics with grace and mutual respect.

Love Languages: Tailoring Affection to Your Partner

Have you ever wondered why certain gestures make you feel more loved than others? The concept of love languages might hold the key. Developed by Dr. Gary Chapman, love languages describe the different ways people express and receive love. There are five primary love languages: words of affirmation, acts of service, receiving gifts, quality time, and physical touch. Each language speaks to a unique aspect of emotional connection. Understanding these can transform how you and your partner show affection, making sure your expressions of love truly resonate. It's like speaking the same language but in the dialect that means the most to each of you.

Try taking an online quiz or assessment to discover your and your partner's love languages. These tools are straightforward and can provide insights into what makes each of you feel most valued. Once you've identified your love languages, the next step is to adapt your expressions of affection accordingly. If your partner's love language is acts of service, simple gestures like making coffee in the morning or taking care of a chore can speak volumes. For those who appreciate receiving gifts, it's not about the price tag but the thoughtfulness behind the gesture. A handwritten note or a small token that shows you've been thinking about them can be incredibly meaningful.

Consider trying a love language challenge to keep things exciting and ensure you're meeting each other's needs. This could be a weekly activity where you swap love languages, practicing each other's preferred form of affection. You might plan a special date night if your language is quality time. Alternatively, if it's a physical touch, a simple hug or a gentle touch can convey deep love and appreciation. These challenges encourage you to step outside your comfort zone, fostering empathy and understanding. Over time, these efforts can lead to a richer, more fulfilling connection. Understanding and practicing each other's love languages can strengthen your bond, creating a deeply tailored relationship with your needs.

CHAPTER 3
EMBRACING DIVERSITY IN
FAITH AND PRACTICE

Maria and David were preparing for a celebration in a small apartment in New York City. Maria, raised in a devout Catholic family, cherished the rituals of midnight Mass and the aroma of incense wafting through the church on Christmas Eve. Coming from a Jewish background, David held dear the lighting of the menorah and the joy of singing traditional Hanukkah songs with his family. As they set their dining table with an eclectic mix of dreidels and nativity scenes, they marveled at how their lives had intertwined to create something uniquely beautiful. The space they share was a testament to their love and respect for each other's traditions, embodying the spirit of togetherness that transcends religious boundaries.

Celebrating different faith traditions begins with acknowledging and respecting each other's beliefs. It's about learning and honoring your partner's important rituals and customs. You can start by researching each other's religious holidays and customs. This might mean understanding Lent's significance in Christianity or Yom Kippur's importance in Judaism. It's about going beyond the surface to appreciate these traditions' deeper meanings. Take the time to visit each other's places of worship or spiritual gatherings. Whether attending a Sunday service or participating in a Shabbat dinner, immersing yourself in your partner's world can offer profound insights into their spiritual life.

Participating actively in each other's religious celebrations is a powerful way to show support and love. Attend major religious festivals together. Whether it's Easter, Diwali, or Eid, being present during these celebrations can strengthen your bond. Consider preparing traditional dishes or decorations for these occasions. Cooking a festive meal or adorning your home with symbols from each tradition can create a warm, inclusive atmosphere. These acts of participation demonstrate a willingness to embrace and celebrate differences, fostering a sense of unity and acceptance.

Sharing the significance of these traditions can deepen your understanding and connection. Engage in storytelling sessions about the history of specific traditions. Discuss the stories behind Christmas, Ramadan, or Passover. Let your partner know why these holidays are special to you and how they shape your spiritual identity. This open dialogue can reveal the values and lessons that each tradition imparts, enriching your relationship with shared knowledge and appreciation. Understanding the stories and meanings behind these celebrations creates a bridge that connects your diverse backgrounds.

Creating inclusive celebrations can be a joyful expression of your shared life. Design celebrations incorporating elements from both traditions, blending them to create unique family customs. Host interfaith gatherings during major holidays. Invite friends and family from both sides to join the festivities, creating a space where everyone feels welcome and respected. Blending traditions might mean having a Christmas tree alongside a menorah or including a Thanksgiving turkey with traditional Indian sweets. These celebrations reflect your shared journey, highlighting the beauty of diversity and the strength of unity.

Interactive Element: Plan an Inclusive Celebration

Objective: Design a celebration that honors both partners' faith traditions.

Instructions:

1. **Choose a Holiday**: Select a holiday that is significant to both partners. It could be a religious holiday, a cultural celebration, or a special occasion.
2. **Research Traditions**: Spend time researching each tradition associated with the holiday. Understand the customs, rituals, and symbols important to each partner.
3. **Plan the Celebration**: Create a plan that incorporates elements from both traditions. Consider the menu, decorations, music, and activities. Aim for a balanced blend that respects and honors both backgrounds.
4. **Invite Guests**: If comfortable, invite friends and family from both sides to participate. Share the significance of each tradition and encourage guests to engage with the diverse elements of the celebration.
5. **Reflect Together**: After the celebration, reflect on the experience. Discuss what went well, what you learned, and how it felt to celebrate together. Use this reflection to inform future celebrations.

By embracing and celebrating different faith traditions, you weave a tapestry of love and respect that enriches your relationship. Through active participation, open dialogue, and inclusive celebrations, you create a shared space where both partners can thrive, honoring their unique identities while building a strong, unified bond.

Finding Common Ground in Diverse Beliefs

Finding common ground can sometimes be a challenge and an opportunity in relationships where partners come from different faith backgrounds. It's less about the differences and more about uncovering the shared values that often lie beneath them. Think of it like sifting through the layers of an onion, where, at the core, you may find mutual beliefs and principles that unite you. Begin by discussing ethical and moral principles that guide your life. Whether it's a commitment to kindness, honesty, or community service, these values are often universal. Focusing on these shared principles creates a foundation that transcends individual religious practices. This foundation strengthens your relationship and promotes a sense of unity and purpose. Once you identify these values, consider creating a shared mission statement for your relationship. This statement is a guiding star, helping you navigate life's challenges together. It encapsulates what you both stand for and aspire to achieve, providing a sense of direction and clarity.

Engaging in regular interfaith dialogues can deepen your understanding of each other's beliefs and spirituality. Set aside time for these conversations, making them a regular part of your relationship. This dedicated time allows for exploration and discovery, encouraging you to ask questions and share experiences. Approach these dialogues with curiosity and openness, focusing on listening rather than debating. It's about creating a safe space where both partners can express their beliefs without fear of judgment. These discussions can reveal insights and perspectives that enrich your relationship, fostering empathy and respect. As you engage in these dialogues, your understanding of each other's faith deepens, leading to a more harmonious and fulfilling partnership.

Developing a unified spiritual vision is a powerful way to respect and honor both belief systems. This vision doesn't mean merging your religious practices but creating a shared understanding of your spiritual goals and aspirations. Drafting a joint spiritual vision or manifesto can be a meaningful exercise. Discuss what spirituality means to each of you and how you can support each other's growth. Consider the role of your beliefs in your relationship and the impact you want them to have on your lives. This vision serves as a roadmap, guiding you as you navigate the complexities of interfaith life. It emphasizes the importance of mutual respect and understanding, allowing both partners to thrive within the relationship.

Practicing empathy and understanding is crucial when navigating diverse beliefs. It's easy to focus on the differences, but empathy allows you to see the world through your partner's eyes. Role-playing exercises can be a helpful tool for building this skill. By stepping into each other's shoes, you gain a deeper appreciation for their perspectives and experiences. This practice fosters compassion and understanding, bridging the gap between differing beliefs.

Additionally, practicing active listening during faith discussions is essential. Focus on genuinely hearing what your partner is saying rather than planning your response. This attentive listening demonstrates respect and validation, reinforcing the importance of their beliefs and experiences. By prioritizing empathy and understanding, you create a relationship environment where both partners feel valued and supported.

In the realm of interfaith relationships, finding common ground is about celebrating both similarities and differences. It's about building a relationship that honors diverse beliefs while nurturing shared values and goals. Through open dialogue, mutual respect, and empathy, you create a partnership enriched by the diversity of your backgrounds. This approach strengthens your bond and enhances your individual spiritual journeys, creating a harmonious and fulfilling relationship that thrives on unity and love.

Shared Rituals and Unique Traditions

Creating shared rituals can be a beautiful way to reflect the rich tapestry of your combined spiritual identities. Imagine starting or ending each day with a ritual celebrating your faith. It might be a morning routine where you light a candle, say a prayer, or read a passage from sacred texts that resonates with both of you. This simple act can set a peaceful tone for the day, reminding you of the strength you draw from your spiritual unity. Or, in the evening, you take a moment to reflect on the day's blessings and challenges, offering gratitude in a way that honors both of your traditions. These rituals don't have to be elaborate. What matters is the intention behind them—a shared acknowledgment of the spiritual bond that holds you together. By crafting rituals that incorporate elements from both faiths, you create a daily practice that is uniquely yours, a testament to the love and respect you have for each other's beliefs.

While shared practices are enriching, preserving your individual traditions is equally important. These personal rituals are vital to your spiritual identity, offering comfort and continuity. Designating special times for individual spiritual practices can help maintain this balance. You could take a few moments each morning for personal reflection or attend a service that speaks to your heart. By honoring these individual practices, you reinforce the unique aspects of your spiritual journey. It's about acknowledging that while you are part of a partnership, you are also individuals with distinct paths. These times of personal reflection can provide insights that you bring back to your shared rituals, enriching them with new perspectives and depth.

Blending rituals can create a meaningful celebration that honors both traditions when significant life events come around. For instance, a wedding or anniversary ceremony can be a beautiful fusion of customs. Consider incorporating readings, music, or symbols from each faith, creating a ceremony that truly represents your partnership. A blended wedding might include a unity ceremony where you light a candle together, combining your individual flames into one. Or you could design a naming ceremony for a child that reflects both of your backgrounds. Such events are about more than just merging traditions; they are about creating new ones that reflect the unique identity of your family. These blended rituals symbolize the harmony and respect you have cultivated, turning life's milestones into celebrations of unity and love.

Reflecting on the evolution of your rituals over time can offer valuable insights into how your relationship has grown. Consider setting aside time during family meetings to discuss how your practices have changed. Talk about the traditions that have persisted and those that have transformed. You may notice that certain rituals have taken on new significance or that others have naturally faded away. This reflection is not about holding onto the past but about acknowledging the journey you've taken together. It's an opportunity to celebrate your relationship's growth and adaptability and to appreciate how you've navigated challenges and embraced change. By looking back on the evolution of your rituals, you gain a deeper understanding of the path you've walked together, strengthening the foundation on which your relationship is built.

Faith-Based Activities for Diverse Couples

When you and your partner have different faith backgrounds, finding shared activities that honor both can be a rewarding experience. Interfaith activities offer an opportunity to explore and sincerely appreciate each other's beliefs. Think about attending interfaith workshops or seminars together. These events bring together people from various faiths to discuss common themes and differences, providing a platform for learning and connection. Such gatherings broaden your understanding and strengthen the bond you share. They encourage open-mindedness and foster a sense of unity, reminding you that, despite differences, much ties us together. Community service projects are another excellent avenue. Choose projects that resonate with your values, whether volunteering at a local shelter or participating in environmental clean-ups. Engaging in these activities aligns with your shared values. It offers a tangible way to live out your faith together, creating shared memories and a sense of accomplishment.

Consider forming or joining interfaith study groups to explore your spiritual perspectives further. These groups create a safe space for discussion and reflection, allowing participants to delve into diverse religious texts and philosophies. Organize a book club focused on interfaith topics, selecting works that challenge and inspire. You and your partner can gain insights into each other's beliefs and discover common ground by reading and discussing these books. It's an exercise in empathy and understanding, encouraging you to see the world through different lenses. Such groups often foster community among participants, providing support and friendship as you navigate your interfaith relationship. These discussions can spark meaningful conversations at home, enriching your relationship with newfound knowledge and understanding.

Joint spiritual practices can be another way to connect on a deeper level. Consider meditation or yoga sessions that honor multiple traditions. These practices promote mindfulness and presence, allowing you to communicate peacefully and intentionally. Look for classes or online resources incorporating elements from both spiritual backgrounds. For instance, a yoga session that includes Christian and Hindu chants or a meditation practice that draws on Buddhist and Islamic teachings. These shared experiences can become a cherished part of your routine, offering tranquility and connection in your busy lives. They remind you that spirituality is a journey you are on together, despite the different paths you may take.

Reflecting on the experiences of engaging in diverse faith activities is crucial for growth. Set aside time to write joint reflections or essays on your interfaith experiences. This practice allows you to process what you've learned and how it's impacted your relationship. Discuss the challenges and triumphs, the moments of insight and understanding. These reflections can serve as a record of your spiritual journey together, a testament to the love and respect you have cultivated. They also provide an opportunity to revisit and reassess your shared goals and aspirations, ensuring your relationship continues growing and evolving. You may discover new areas of connection and understanding as you reflect, further strengthening your bond.

Engaging in faith-based activities can remind us of our shared humanity in a world that often emphasizes our differences. They offer a chance to learn, grow, and connect as individuals and as a couple. By embracing these opportunities, you create a rich, diverse relationship grounded in love. It's about finding harmony in your differences and celebrating the unique tapestry of your shared life. These activities enhance your spiritual connection and enrich your relationship, creating a resilient, compassionate, and deeply fulfilling partnership. As you move forward, keep exploring these avenues of connection, knowing that each step you take together strengthens the foundation of your relationship.

By building diverse spiritual activities, you enrich your shared life with depth and understanding. These practices foster empathy, connection, and growth, enhancing your bond and deepening your love. As you explore these avenues, remember that your journey together is unique and beautiful. Your shared life is a tapestry of experiences woven with threads of faith and understanding. As you move on to the next chapter, you will discover more ways to nurture your relationship, building on the foundation you've created here.

CHAPTER 4
INTEGRATING DEVOTION INTO DAILY LIFE

I magine a couple, Alex and Jamie, who decided to make devotion a daily habit. They both have demanding jobs and a lively household, so finding time for each other, let alone spiritual practices, seemed impossible. One evening, they sat together and decided to carve out a few minutes each day for devotionals. They started with a simple commitment—a five-minute reflection before bed. Slowly, this small routine became a cherished part of their day, a moment of peace amidst the chaos. Their bond strengthened, and they found themselves more connected, not only to each other but also to their faith. This chapter is all about creating those moments for you and your partner.

Establishing a routine for your devotionals is key to making them a lasting part of your life. Devotionals can become a daily ritual, like brushing your teeth or having your morning coffee. Start by setting aside a specific time each day. It doesn't have to be lengthy—five minutes can be enough. Choose a time that suits both of you, whether early morning, during lunch, or before bed. Consistency is crucial, so consider setting a shared calendar reminder. This way, you'll have a gentle nudge to keep your commitment, ensuring that devotionals are integral to your day.

Starting small is important for sustainability. If you dive into hour-long sessions immediately, you might find it overwhelming and hard to maintain. Begin with short, focused sessions. Five-minute devotionals can be a great way to ease into the habit. Over time, as you grow more comfortable, you might naturally extend these sessions. The key is to build gradually, allowing your devotional practice to grow at a pace that feels right for both of you. This approach fosters sustainability and helps prevent burnout, ensuring your practice remains enjoyable and fulfilling.

Creating a supportive environment is essential for a successful devotional routine. Find a quiet space where you can focus without distractions. It might be a cozy corner of your living room or a peaceful spot in your garden. The environment should feel inviting and conducive to reflection. Consider using calming scents like lavender or soft lighting to create a tranquil atmosphere. This dedicated space can become your sanctuary, where you both feel at ease and connected. Eliminating distractions allows you to be fully present, enhancing the quality of your devotional time together.

Tracking your progress can be a great motivator. Consider using a devotional journal or an app to record your reflections and experiences. This practice allows you to look back and see how far you've come, celebrating your consistency and growth. It also provides an opportunity to identify patterns and areas for improvement. Whether you choose a traditional journal or a digital app, the act of tracking can deepen your commitment and enhance your devotional practice. Celebrating milestones, no matter how small, reinforces the positive impact of your efforts, encouraging you to continue nurturing your spiritual connection.

Interactive Element: Devotional Progress Tracker

Objective: Keep track of your devotional practice and celebrate your progress.

Instructions:

1. **Choose a Tracking Method**: Decide whether you prefer a traditional journal or a digital app. The YouVersion Bible App is a great choice, offering features like note-sharing and reminders.
2. **Set Goals**: Establish small, achievable goals for your devotional practice. One goal could be completing a week of daily reflections or trying a new devotional format.
3. **Record Your Sessions**: After each devotional, take a moment to jot down your reflections. Note any insights, challenges, or feelings that arise.
4. **Review Regularly**: Set aside time each month to review your entries. Reflect on your progress and celebrate the milestones you've reached.
5. **Adjust as Needed**: Use your reflections to make necessary adjustments to your routine, ensuring it remains engaging and fulfilling.

By integrating these steps into your life, you can create a meaningful and sustainable devotional practice. This approach strengthens your spiritual connection and enriches your relationship, providing a foundation for growth and unity.

Quick Devotions: Spiritual Growth for Busy Schedules

Picture this: You're rushing through your morning, juggling work emails and preparing breakfast, when you remember you only have a minute before the day kicks off. It's easy to assume that something so short can't make a difference. Still, brief, focused devotionals bring clarity and peace, even on the busiest days. Quick devotions serve as a spiritual reset, a moment to center yourself amidst the chaos. They can bring mental clarity and remind you of the bigger picture, grounding you in your values and intentions. These moments of reflection can be just as nourishing as longer sessions, offering a touchstone of calm in an otherwise hectic schedule.

Developing short devotional practices is all about finding those snippets of time that often go unnoticed. A "One-Minute Prayer" might be just what you need to start or end your day with intention. Take a deep breath, focus on a single thought or intention, and offer it in prayer. It's a small act but can set a positive tone for everything that follows. If you commute by public transport or even drive a familiar route, use that time for scripture meditation. Choose a passage that resonates with you, and spend a few moments reflecting on its meaning. This practice enriches your spiritual life and turns routine moments into opportunities for growth and reflection.

Identifying key moments for devotion throughout your day is easier than it seems. Look at your schedule and pinpoint times when you can incorporate spiritual practices without disrupting your flow. Lunchtime reflections, for instance, are a great way to pause and recharge mid-day. You don't need much—just a quiet corner to focus on a single thought or scripture. Similarly, waiting in line can transform into a meditative moment. Instead of scrolling through your phone, take a breath and reflect on a passage or prayer. These small windows of time add up, providing a series of touchpoints that connect you to your faith and each other.

The depth of your quick devotions matters more than their length. It's about the intention behind the practice, not the duration. Selecting impactful scripture passages can make all the difference. Choose verses that speak to your current situation or challenge you to think in new ways. Reflect on their meaning and how they apply to your life. This approach ensures that even the shortest devotional carries weight and significance. It's a mindfulness practice, focusing on quality over quantity, allowing you to engage deeply with your faith in a way that fits your lifestyle.

Interactive Element: Scripture Meditation Guide

Objective: Integrate scripture meditation into daily routines for spiritual growth.

Instructions:

1. **Select a Passage**: Choose a verse or passage that resonates with you. It could be something relevant to your current situation or a favorite that brings comfort.
2. **Find a Moment**: Identify a time during your day when you can focus, such as during your commute or lunch break.
3. **Meditate**: Spend a minute or two reflecting on the passage. Consider its meaning and how it applies to your life. Allow the words to settle into your mind and heart.
4. **Reflect**: After your meditation, take a moment to jot down any insights or thoughts that arise. Use these reflections to guide your actions and mindset throughout the day.

By weaving quick devotions into your routine, you enrich your spiritual life and create moments of connection and clarity that elevate your daily experience.

Digital Devotionals: Utilizing Technology for Spiritual Growth

Integrating technology into your spiritual practice can open possibilities in today's digital age. Imagine having access to daily scripture readings and reflections, ready to provide insight and inspiration whenever needed. Digital tools like mobile apps offer this convenience, making it easier than ever to incorporate devotionals into your life. For instance, the "YouVersion Bible App" is a treasure trove of resources, offering a vast library of devotions tailored to couples. With a tap, you can explore passages that speak to your situation, share notes with your partner, and even set reminders to keep you on track. This accessibility turns what might feel like a daunting task into a seamless part of your daily routine.

Choosing the right digital resources is crucial to support your spiritual goals and preferences. Not every app or online community will suit your needs, so take the time to explore what's out there. Popular devotional apps like "Gottman Card Decks" and "Love Nudge" can enhance your experience by fostering communication and aligning with your love languages. As you review these options, consider what resonates with both of you. Do you prefer guided reflections, or do you want something that encourages discussion? Evaluating online devotional communities can also provide support and connection. These platforms offer a space to share experiences and insights with others on a similar spiritual path, enriching your practice with diverse perspectives.

Multimedia elements can add depth and variety to your devotional time. Imagine listening to an audio devotional during your morning workout, letting the words guide your thoughts as you start the day. You and your partner may enjoy watching inspirational videos, sparking conversations that deepen your understanding and connection. Incorporating multimedia resources allows you to engage with your faith in new and dynamic ways, breaking the mold of traditional practices. It's about creating an experience that resonates on multiple levels, engaging your senses and emotions. Mixing things up keeps your practice fresh and meaningful, ensuring it remains an integral part of your relationship.

However, as beneficial as technology can be, it's important to maintain a healthy balance. The convenience of digital tools can sometimes overshadow the need for unplugged, focused time together. Consider setting tech-free zones during your devotionals, where phones and devices are put aside to allow uninterrupted connection. This boundary ensures that your spiritual practice remains sacred, free from the distractions of the digital world. Establishing these zones can enhance the quality of your interactions, allowing you to be fully present with each other and your shared faith. It's a reminder that while technology is a valuable tool, the heart of your practice lies in the connection you cultivate.

While technology offers many benefits, it's easy to become reliant on it, potentially diminishing your practice's personal and intimate aspects. To counter this, create moments where you engage with each other directly, without the mediation of screens or apps. These times allow for organic growth and reflection, fostering a deeper, more personal connection. By striking this balance, you can enjoy the advantages of digital devotionals while preserving the authenticity and warmth of your spiritual journey as a couple.

Morning Rituals: Starting the Day with Intention

There's something magical about the early morning hours when the world is still quiet and the day is full of potential. Crafting morning devotional rituals can transform these moments into a sacred time for connection and growth. Begin with a simple scripture reading and reflection. Choose a passage that resonates with both of you, perhaps something that speaks to what you're currently experiencing or a verse that inspires hope and gratitude. As you read, take turns sharing your thoughts and feelings. This practice grounds you spiritually and sets a positive tone for the day, fostering a sense of unity and purpose.

Incorporating mindfulness and prayer into your morning routine enhances focus and intention. Consider starting with guided morning prayers that help center your thoughts and align your intentions. These prayers can be brief, offering peace before the day's activities begin. Pair this with mindful breathing exercises to cultivate presence and calm. A few deep breaths can clear your mind and prepare you for whatever the day holds. These practices encourage you to enter the day with a clear mind and an open heart, ready to embrace challenges and celebrate joys together.

Personalizing your morning rituals ensures they resonate deeply with both of you. Align these practices with your rhythms, adjusting them to fit your unique preferences and lifestyle. If you love music, try customizing a morning playlist with worship songs that uplift your spirit. Let these melodies fill your space, creating an atmosphere of joy and reflection. This personalization makes the ritual feel authentic and enjoyable, something you look forward to each morning. It's about finding what works for you as a couple and making it a cherished part of your day.

Evaluating the impact of your morning devotions is key to maintaining their effectiveness. Set aside time each week to check in with each other about your devotional satisfaction. Discuss what's working well and what might need adjustment. A particular scripture spoke to you, or a practice didn't resonate as expected. These conversations allow you to fine-tune your routine, ensuring it remains meaningful and fulfilling. Regularly assessing your rituals keeps them fresh and aligned with your evolving spiritual needs, allowing your morning devotionals to grow and adapt.

Evening Reflections: Ending the Day with Gratitude

As the day draws to a close and the world quiets down, it's the perfect time to settle into an evening reflection routine that fosters gratitude and connection. Picture this: you and your partner, relaxing in a cozy spot, perhaps on the couch or in bed, with a notebook in hand. This is your time to unwind, to reflect on the day's events, and to express thanks for the moments that brought joy or insight. Evening gratitude journaling can be a simple practice where you jot down a few things you're thankful for. It doesn't have to be grand—sometimes, the little things matter most, like a shared laugh over dinner or a kind word from a stranger. By documenting these moments, you create a record of daily blessings that you can reflect on, reinforcing a positive mindset and nurturing your relationship.

Sharing daily highs and lows with your partner can deepen this connection. It's a chance to openly communicate what went well and what might have been challenging. This practice encourages empathy and understanding as you listen and support each other's experiences. By acknowledging the highs, you celebrate together; by sharing the lows, you offer comfort and solidarity. This exchange strengthens your emotional bond and fosters a sense of partnership, reminding you that you're in this together.

Incorporating scripture and prayer into your evening reflections reinforces your faith and connection. Consider reading a psalm together each night, allowing its words to soothe your mind and spirit. The Psalms offer a range of emotions and insights, from joy and gratitude to lament and hope, providing a rich tapestry of reflections for any mood or situation. Pair this with bedtime prayers for peace, where you both take a moment to express your hopes and intentions for the night and the day to come. These practices create a spiritual anchor, grounding you in your faith and partnership as you prepare to rest.

Creating a calming atmosphere is key to setting the stage for these evening rituals. As the evening unfolds, dim the lights to create a relaxed ambiance. Consider using calming scents like lavender or chamomile, known for their soothing properties, to enhance the sense of tranquility. These small touches transform your space into a haven of peace, inviting you to slow down and savor the moment. The environment you cultivate reflects your commitment to each other and your shared spiritual journey.

Reflecting on daily blessings is a powerful way to end the day on a positive note. Consider forming a gratitude-sharing circle with your family, where everyone can express their gratitude. This practice strengthens family bonds and instills a sense of appreciation and mindfulness in your home. As you acknowledge these blessings, you shift your focus from what might be lacking to what is abundant, reinforcing a mindset of gratitude and contentment.

Integrating these evening reflection practices into your routine creates a sacred space for connection, gratitude, and faith. These moments become a cherished part of your day, offering a sense of closure and peace as you prepare for rest. As you continue exploring these practices, remember that they are not about perfection but presence and intention. Each evening offers a new opportunity to reflect, connect, and grow together, deepening your bond and nurturing your shared spiritual life.

In the quiet of the evening, as you breathe in the calm and reflect on the day's blessings, you lay the foundation for a stronger, more connected relationship. The practices you cultivate here are not just about ending the day well—they are about building a life rich in gratitude, love, and faith. With each reflection, you reinforce the threads that bind you, preparing for the new day and the new chapter that awaits.

REVIEW

Help Us Spread Love and Connection

Your Voice Can Make a Difference

"The best way to find yourself is to lose yourself in the service of others." - Mahatma Gandhi

Life is full of ups and downs, but love and faith help us find steady ground. When you give selflessly—even just your thoughts—you create a ripple effect of kindness and hope.

Would you help another couple searching for deeper connection and faith?

Our mission with *Relationship Devotional for Couples* is to make building strong, faith-filled relationships easier and more meaningful for everyone. But we can't do it alone.

Most couples discover books like this through honest reviews. That's where you come in.

Your review could inspire a couple to take the first step toward growing closer to each other and God. Imagine what your words could do:

- One more couple reconnects after a hard season.
- One more family finds peace in the chaos of life.
- One more relationship is strengthened through faith.

Writing a review costs nothing and takes just a minute, but its impact could be life-changing for someone else.

To share your thoughts, simply scan the QR code below or visit:

[https://www.amazon.com/review/review-your-purchases/?asin=BOOKASIN]

If you love supporting others and spreading love, you're exactly the kind of person this world needs. Thank you, from the bottom of my heart, for helping us reach more hearts and homes.

With gratitude,

Dean Ramsey

CHAPTER 5
NAVIGATING LIFE TRANSITIONS TOGETHER

When Emma and Jake found out they were expecting their first child, excitement quickly mingled with uncertainty. They knew becoming parents would change everything, but they hadn't anticipated how it would alter their relationship. Suddenly, their world was a whirlwind of nursery colors, parenting books, and well-meaning advice from every corner. As they prepared for this new chapter, they realized the importance of facing transitions together, hand in hand. Whether anticipated or unforeseen, life transitions can reshape your relationship's landscape. They touch every aspect of your life, from daily routines to emotional well-being. Whether it's the joyful chaos of welcoming a new baby, the upheaval of a career change, or the adventure of moving to a new city, these shifts bring challenges and growth opportunities.

Understanding the nature of transitions is the first step in navigating them. These periods of change can affect your relationship unexpectedly, testing your resilience and communication skills. Transitions often bring stress and uncertainty as they disrupt the familiar patterns that make life feel secure. For example, becoming a parent is a joyful milestone but also demands adjustments in roles and responsibilities. Similarly, career changes can lead to financial strain or shifts in identity, while relocating might challenge your sense of community and belonging. Recognizing these impacts can help you prepare mentally and emotionally, ensuring you face these changes as a united front.

Proactive transition preparation can ease the journey. Start by creating a transition timeline, outlining key milestones and tasks. This roadmap provides a clear view of what lies ahead, reducing the chaos that often accompanies change. Identify potential challenges and brainstorm solutions. Suppose you're moving to a new city and research neighborhoods, schools, and amenities together. For a career change, consider the financial implications and explore alternative income sources. By anticipating these hurdles, you equip yourselves with the tools to navigate them smoothly. This preparation reduces stress and empowers you to approach transitions with confidence and clarity.

Communication during transitions is crucial. Open dialogue allows you to express concerns, share hopes, and align your expectations. Schedule regular check-in conversations to discuss your progress and feelings. These check-ins create a safe space for vulnerability, encouraging honest discussions that strengthen your bond. Active listening techniques, such as reflecting on your partner's words, can enhance understanding and empathy. During these talks, focus on expressing your thoughts clearly and listening openly. This communication fosters a sense of partnership, reminding you you're on this journey together.

Building resilience together is key to adapting to change. Joint stress-relief activities, like yoga or long walks, can offer respite and relaxation. These shared experiences bring you closer, allowing you to reset and recharge. Additionally, consider building a support network of friends, family, or community groups. These connections offer encouragement and advice, bolstering your resilience during challenging times. They remind you that you're not alone, providing a sense of belonging and support. By fostering resilience, you equip yourselves to face transitions with strength and optimism, ensuring your relationship thrives through change.

Interactive Element: Transition Timeline

Objective: Create a visual timeline to navigate life transitions smoothly.

Instructions:

1. **Identify the Transition**: Whether you're moving, making a career change, or starting a family, clearly define the transition you're preparing for.
2. **Outline Key Milestones**: Break down the transition into smaller, manageable steps. Include important dates, tasks, and goals.
3. **Anticipate Challenges**: List potential obstacles you might face and brainstorm solutions together.
4. **Assign Responsibilities**: Determine who will handle each task, ensuring a balanced workload.
5. **Please review and Adjust**: Regularly revisit your timeline, updating it as needed to reflect changes or new developments.

Creating a transition timeline can provide clarity and direction, reduce stress, and foster a sense of control as you navigate life's changes. By working together, you strengthen your partnership, ensuring you face these transitions confidently and in unity.

Career Shifts: Supporting Professional Growth

Recognizing when a career shift might benefit you or your partner can sometimes be tricky. However, signs often indicate it might be time for a change. Perhaps you're feeling restless or uninspired by your current role. Stress has become a constant companion, creeping into your evenings and weekends. Or, you might notice a lack of fulfillment, a sensation that your work no longer aligns with your values or aspirations. Identifying these signs is crucial, as they signal that your career is not just a job but a vital part of your overall satisfaction and well-being. Regularly evaluating your career goals and aspirations can help ensure that your path remains aligned with what truly matters to you. This might involve reflecting on what you enjoy most or considering what new skills or experiences you wish to gain. By staying attuned to these signs, you can proactively address career dissatisfaction before it escalates into a broader issue, impacting your professional life and your personal relationships.

Supporting each other's career goals requires a blend of encouragement and practical assistance. Start by openly discussing your partner's ambitions and how you can be a part of their journey. Creating a career development plan together can be an enlightening exercise. It helps both of you get on the same page about short-term goals and long-term aspirations. This plan might include setting specific milestones, identifying necessary skills or training, and outlining potential career paths. Offering emotional support is equally important. Be there to listen without judgment and celebrate their successes, no matter how small. Providing logistical support, like extra household duties during a busy period, can also make a significant difference. By actively participating in each other's growth, you foster a partnership built on mutual respect and shared dreams.

Juggling career ambitions with relationship commitments is an ongoing challenge. It often feels like a tightrope walk, where maintaining balance is key. Implement effective time management techniques to create space for both. This might mean setting clear boundaries around work hours to protect your personal time. You could establish a rule that after 7 PM, work emails are off-limits, or weekends are reserved for family and relaxation. Prioritizing quality time with each other can prevent your relationship from taking a backseat. Plan regular date nights or weekend getaways, ensuring your connection remains a priority amidst work demands. It's about creating a rhythm that honors both your professional and personal lives, ensuring neither is neglected.

Navigating job loss or career setbacks can be a daunting experience. Still, with the proper support, it can become an opportunity for growth. When faced with unexpected career challenges, approach them with empathy and understanding. Coping mechanisms like maintaining a routine, engaging in physical activity, or practicing mindfulness can help manage stress and maintain perspective. Exploring new opportunities together can also be a rewarding process. Sit down with your partner and brainstorm paths aligning with their skills and passions. Please encourage them to pursue interests that may have been previously sidelined. This exploration opens doors to new possibilities and reinforces your support and commitment to each other's happiness and success. By facing these challenges as a team, you strengthen your relationship, turning setbacks into stepping stones for future endeavors.

Parenting Partnership: Navigating Family Dynamics

Stepping into parenthood is like entering a new world filled with joy, challenges, and endless possibilities. It's a time when you and your partner will grow in ways you've never imagined, but it also requires preparation. One of the first steps is creating a parenting plan. This isn't just about logistics, like who handles midnight feedings or pediatrician appointments; it's about establishing a shared vision for how you want to raise your child. Discuss values, discipline approaches, and education preferences. By aligning on these big-picture ideas, you set a strong foundation. Attending parenting classes together can also be incredibly beneficial. These sessions offer practical advice, but more importantly, they provide a space to learn and grow as a team. You'll walk away with confidence and a toolkit of strategies to handle whatever comes your way.

Once your little one arrives, co-parenting strategies become crucial. Effective co-parenting is all about partnership and shared responsibilities. Discuss and agree on how to divide parenting duties. One of you is a morning person and handles breakfast and school drop-offs. At the same time, the other takes on bedtime stories and weekend activities. A clear division of labor helps prevent burnout and ensures both partners feel valued and involved. Consistent communication about parenting decisions is vital. Regularly check in to discuss what's working and what could be improved. Approach these conversations with openness and flexibility, understanding that parenting is dynamic. By fostering collaboration, you create an environment where both partners can thrive as parents.

Amidst the demands of parenting, maintaining relationship intimacy might feel challenging, but it's essential. Scheduling regular date nights can help keep the spark alive. These don't have to be elaborate; even a simple meal at home can be unique if you're intentional about the time you share. Use these moments to reconnect, talk about things other than parenting, and remind each other why you fell in love. Practicing gratitude and appreciation daily can also strengthen your bond. Please take a moment each day to express what you appreciate about your partner, whether it's their patience, humor, or how they make your child laugh. These small gestures reinforce your connection, ensuring your relationship remains a priority.

As families grow, dynamics inevitably change. Adapting to these shifts requires patience and communication, whether welcoming a new family member or adjusting to children leaving home. Family meetings can be an effective tool for open discussions. Use these gatherings to discuss changes, address concerns, and celebrate achievements. They're a great way to involve everyone, ensuring each family member feels heard and valued. Celebrating family milestones, like birthdays, graduations, or even the first day of school, can strengthen family bonds. These celebrations don't just mark important moments; they create memories that bring everyone closer together. Embrace these changes as opportunities to grow and evolve as a family, knowing that you're building a stronger, more resilient unit with every transition.

Relocation Realities: Maintaining Connection Amidst Moves

Relocating can feel like stepping into a new world filled with unknowns and fresh possibilities. Whether it's a move across town or to an entirely new city, the logistics of packing up your life and starting anew can be daunting. Planning plays a crucial role in easing the transition. Begin by researching new locations together. Explore different neighborhoods, considering factors like proximity to work, schools, and community amenities. This research can be a fun way to imagine your new life and align your vision. Next, create a moving checklist to keep everything organized. List tasks like hiring movers, transferring utilities, and updating your address. This checklist serves as a roadmap, ensuring nothing gets overlooked during the hectic process of relocation.

Adjusting to a new environment takes time and patience. Once you've settled in, take the opportunity to explore your new area together. Walk around the neighborhood, visit local parks, and try nearby cafes. This helps you become familiar with your surroundings and creates shared experiences that strengthen your bond. Joining local groups or activities can also enhance your sense of belonging. Whether it's a book club, sports team, or volunteer organization, participating in community events allows you to meet new people and build connections. These activities provide a support network, making your new location feel more like home.

Sometimes, relocation means temporary separation due to work commitments or other circumstances. Maintaining connections in long-distance relationships requires effort and creativity. Regular virtual date nights can be a great way to bridge the gap. Set a specific time each week to connect via video call, share a meal, or watch a movie together despite the miles between you. Sending care packages or letters adds a personal touch, reminding each other of your love and commitment. These gestures keep the romance alive, ensuring that distance doesn't weaken the bond you share.

Instead of viewing relocation as a daunting task, see it as an adventure filled with potential for growth and new experiences. Embrace the opportunity to explore local culture and cuisine. Try new foods, attend cultural festivals, and learn about the history and traditions of your new area. These explorations enrich your life, offering a deeper understanding of the place you now call home. Additionally, this move will be a chance to set new personal and joint goals. You may take up a new hobby, learn a language, or set fitness targets. These goals provide a sense of direction and purpose, helping you make the most of your new beginning.

Retirement Readiness: Redefining Roles and Goals

As you stand on the brink of retirement, it's like looking out at a vast open sea, full of potential. It's a time to redefine what the next chapter of life will look like together. One of the first steps is planning for retirement, a crucial aspect that covers financial stability and emotional and relational well-being. Creating a retirement savings plan is essential, ensuring both feel secure about the future. Sit down and examine your financial landscape—look at savings, investments, and potential income sources. This planning isn't just about numbers; it's about aligning your financial situation with your shared dreams and goals. Maybe it's traveling the world or simply enjoying quiet mornings with coffee. Identifying these shared retirement goals gives you a vision to work towards, making those dreams tangible and achievable.

Retirement brings a shift in roles and responsibilities, an exciting and challenging dynamic. With more time on your hands, there's an opportunity to explore new hobbies and interests together. Perhaps you've always wanted to take up gardening, painting, or even learning a new language. These shared activities fill your days with joy and strengthen your connection as you discover new facets of each other. Alongside this exploration, sharing household responsibilities becomes more significant. With both of you at home, it's crucial to communicate and decide how tasks will be divided. This collaboration fosters a sense of teamwork, preventing one partner from feeling overwhelmed or underappreciated. You create a harmonious environment that reflects your new lifestyle by redefining these roles.

Maintaining a vibrant relationship during retirement is essential to keep things engaging and fulfilling. Whether local travel or exploring places you've always dreamed of visiting, pursue new adventures together. These shared experiences create lasting memories, adding richness to your relationship. Additionally, consider participating in community service. Volunteering gives back to the community and provides a sense of purpose and connection beyond yourselves. It's an opportunity to meet new people and engage in meaningful activities, keeping your days interesting and rewarding. These pursuits enrich your relationship, ensuring retirement is a time of growth and discovery.

Embracing the retirement transition involves reflecting on life achievements and setting intentions for the future. Take time to celebrate what you've accomplished individually and as a couple. These reflections highlight the strengths and resilience that have brought you to this point. As you look back, also think about what lies ahead. Setting intentions for the future provides direction and motivation, guiding you in this new phase of life. Consider what you want to achieve, learn, or experience in this newfound freedom. Whether it's deepening your spiritual practice, fostering creative endeavors, or simply enjoying the tranquility of each day, these intentions shape a retirement that is fulfilling and aligned with your values.

As you step into this new chapter, remember that retirement is about more than just leaving the workforce; it's about embracing the opportunities it brings. Each moment is a chance to redefine your relationship, explore new passions, and live with intention. Planning together ensures that this phase of life is filled with joy, connection, and purpose. The journey ahead is yours to shape, offering endless possibilities for growth and happiness.

As we conclude this chapter on navigating life's transitions, we've touched on the importance of planning, communication, and embracing change. Whether preparing for retirement or adjusting to new family dynamics, these transitions offer opportunities for growth and deeper connection. In the upcoming chapter, we'll look at building a positive and supportive environment, ensuring your relationship thrives in every season of life.

CHAPTER 6
FINANCIAL HARMONY AND PLANNING

Picture this: Sam and Alex, a young couple just starting their marriage, were tangled in a web of financial misunderstandings. Sam loved to save for a rainy day, while Alex enjoyed spontaneous weekend getaways. Their differing views on money often led to heated discussions, making them realize the need for a more structured approach to managing their finances. They decided to implement regular financial check-ins, and this simple change transformed their bank statements and relationships. By setting aside time each month to discuss their finances, they created a shared vision for their future, aligning their financial goals with mutual dreams and priorities.

Financial Check-In: Regular Money Conversations

The key to financial harmony is establishing a routine for financial discussions. Like Sam and Alex, scheduling regular financial check-ins can help you stay aligned and address concerns. Consider setting a monthly financial review meeting where you both come prepared with a financial agenda. This structured approach ensures you cover all necessary topics, from monthly expenses to long-term savings goals. Having these meetings regularly keeps financial matters from piling up and becoming overwhelming. It's like a monthly tune-up for your financial health, ensuring everything runs smoothly and efficiently.

Creating a safe space for money talks is crucial. Money can be sensitive, but fostering an open, non-judgmental environment can make all the difference. Establish ground rules for your discussions, such as taking turns speaking or refraining from interrupting. This structure helps maintain focus and respect, allowing both partners to express their thoughts and concerns freely. Utilize active listening to ensure that each partner feels heard and understood. This means putting down your phone, making eye contact, and summarizing your partner's words to confirm understanding. These practices create a supportive environment where financial conversations can flourish.

Setting financial goals together is another step in achieving financial harmony. It's essential to identify what you both want to accomplish with your money, whether saving for a dream vacation, buying a home, or planning for retirement. Engage in short-term and long-term goal-setting exercises to clarify your priorities. You could start with a short-term goal like building an emergency fund, then move on to longer-term ambitions like investing for retirement. These exercises help align your financial aspirations, ensuring you work toward the same objectives. Setting these goals together strengthens your partnership and creates a shared vision for your financial future.

Once you have your goals in place, tracking financial progress becomes essential. Monitoring your progress helps you stay on track and make adjustments as needed. Consider using budgeting apps like YNAB or Mint to monitor your spending and savings. These tools provide an overview of your financial situation, making it easier to see where your money goes and where you can improve. Creating a financial progress chart can also be beneficial.

Visualizing your progress can be motivating, reminding you how far you've come and where you want to go. Regularly reviewing your financial status lets you gain insight into your habits and make informed decisions to achieve your goals.

Interactive Element: Financial Progress Chart

Objective: Track financial goals and progress visually to stay motivated and aligned.

Instructions:

1. **Create a Chart**: Use a whiteboard, spreadsheet, or app to create a chart with columns for goals, current status, and target dates.
2. **Set Goals**: List all financial goals, categorizing them as short-term or long-term.
3. **Track Progress**: Update the chart regularly with your progress, noting improvements or setbacks.
4. **Review Together**: Review the chart during your financial check-ins, discussing any adjustments needed.
5. **Celebrate Milestones**: Mark milestones with small celebrations to acknowledge achievements and stay motivated.

By incorporating these practices, you can achieve financial harmony and strengthen your relationship. Regular financial check-ins, open communication, and shared goals can transform how you manage money, making it a positive force in your partnership.

Budgeting as a Team: Aligning Financial Goals

Creating a budget together is like drawing a roadmap for your financial future. It's about balancing both partners' needs and dreams to ensure you're heading in the same direction. Start with joint budget planning sessions. These are dedicated times when you both outline your financial landscape. Look at your income, assess your expenses, and identify areas for adjustments. This process helps you understand each other's financial habits and preferences. It's not just about numbers; it's a chance to connect over shared goals and aspirations. One of you is more focused on saving for a future home, while the other prioritizes paying off student loans. By having these discussions, you align your financial goals, creating a cohesive plan that reflects your priorities.

Once you have a basic framework, you'll need to prioritize expenses. This involves distinguishing between what you need and what you want. Needs are those non-negotiables like rent, utilities, and groceries. Wants are the extras, like dining out or that new gadget you've been eyeing. A needs vs. wants analysis helps you allocate funds wisely, ensuring that essentials are covered before indulging in extras. It's not about depriving yourselves but making conscious choices that support your financial health. As you discuss these categories, you might discover areas where you can cut back, freeing up resources for more important goals. This exercise encourages transparency and cooperation, turning budgeting into a team effort rather than a solo endeavor.

Budgets aren't set in stone. Life happens, and it's crucial to adjust your budget dynamically to accommodate changes in income or expenses. One of you may get a raise, or an unexpected medical bill may come up. Flexibility is key. Developing strategies for reallocating funds during financial shifts ensures you're prepared for the unexpected. You can reduce discretionary spending or adjust your savings contributions temporarily. Being adaptable helps you navigate these changes without derailing your overall financial plan. It's about staying proactive and responsive, ensuring that your budget remains a living document that evolves with your circumstances.

Celebrating budget successes is an often overlooked but vital part of the process. Acknowledging and celebrating your achievements reinforces positive behavior and keeps you motivated. Set up a reward system for meeting budget milestones. It could be a special dinner, a small treat, or even a day off from budgeting discussions. These celebrations don't have to be extravagant; what matters is the recognition of your hard work and dedication. Celebrating together reinforces that budgeting isn't just about restriction and achieving your shared dreams and goals. It's a reminder that you're in this together, supporting each other every step of the way.

Saving and Spending: Balancing Present and Future Needs

Understanding the importance of saving is like building a safety net that catches you when life throws a curveball. Savings are crucial for security and reaching those dreams that keep you motivated. Consider an emergency fund as your financial cushion, a buffer against unexpected expenses like car repairs or medical bills. Aim to save at least three to six months of living expenses. This might sound daunting, but breaking it into smaller, achievable goals makes it manageable. Imagine the peace of mind that comes with knowing you can handle an emergency without stress. This cushion isn't just about security; it's about freedom, allowing you to make decisions without fear of financial strain.

Creating a savings plan that aligns with your goals involves planning and cooperation. Consider using automated savings strategies to make the process easier. Automatic transfers from your checking account to savings can help you build your fund without thinking about it. Set savings targets for specific goals, like a vacation or a down payment for a house. These targets keep you focused and motivated. Picture a chart on your fridge, tracking your progress toward that dream vacation. Each dollar saved gets you closer, turning saving into a rewarding experience rather than a chore. The key is to ensure that your savings plan reflects both partners' aspirations, reinforcing your shared future.

Balancing enjoyment and prudence in spending is all about finding that sweet spot where you can live in the moment without jeopardizing your financial health. Life is meant to be enjoyed, and indulging occasionally is okay. But how do you want today while preparing for tomorrow? Start by setting clear discretionary spending guidelines. Allocate a portion of your budget for fun activities, like dining out or catching a movie. Explore budget-friendly activities that bring joy without breaking the bank—think picnics in the park or game nights at home. It's about making memories without the guilt that comes from overspending. By being mindful of your spending, you ensure you live within your means while savoring life's pleasures.

Evaluating spending habits regularly helps keep you on track and aligned with your financial goals. Set aside time each month for a spending reflection exercise. Look at where your money went and consider whether it aligns with your priorities. Did you spend more time dining out than planned? Were there unexpected expenses that need addressing? Reflect on these questions together, discussing what worked and what didn't. This reflection isn't about shaming or blaming but understanding and adjusting. Use this time to celebrate successes and make necessary changes, ensuring that your spending supports your goals rather than undermines them. Regular reflection fosters transparency and accountability, strengthening your financial partnership.

Handling Financial Stress: Strategies for Peace

Stress around money can be a heavy load to carry. It's not just about numbers and bank statements; the emotion tied to those digits can weigh you down. Recognizing the sources of this stress is the first step to finding relief. Debt is often a major culprit. It lingers in the background, casting a shadow over your financial landscape. Tackling it head-on requires a strategy. Start by listing all your debts, from credit cards to student loans. Identify which carries the highest interest rates and consider focusing on paying those off first. Some folks find the "snowball method" helpful—first paying down the smallest debts to gain momentum and confidence. Each small victory can lift some of the burden off your shoulders, making the more enormous debts feel a bit more manageable.

Managing financial stress also means developing coping mechanisms that protect your emotional well-being. Mindfulness exercises can be efficient. Simple practices like deep breathing or guided meditation can help calm the mind, provide clarity, and reduce anxiety. Picture a few deep breaths as a reset button, allowing you to approach financial challenges with a fresh perspective. In addition to mindfulness, consider reaching out to support groups. Whether online or in-person, sharing your experiences with others in similar situations can provide comfort and new insights. Knowing you're not alone in your struggles can be incredibly reassuring. It may even lead to valuable advice that you hadn't considered.

Financial resilience is another piece of the puzzle. It's about building up your defenses so that when financial challenges arise, you're better equipped to handle them. One way to do this is by diversifying your income streams. You may have a hobby that could turn into a side hustle, or you can take on freelance work in your field. Additional income can provide a buffer, reducing stress and increasing financial security. Establishing a financial safety net, such as an emergency fund, is crucial to resilience. This fund provides a cushion, allowing you to tackle unexpected expenses without derailing your financial plan. Even a small monthly contribution can build up over time, giving peace of mind.

Open communication becomes crucial when you face financial strain. It's easy to let stress create barriers between you and your partner, but maintaining dialogue is key to navigating these challenges together. Use conflict resolution techniques to guide your conversations. This might involve setting rules for discussions, such as taking turns speaking or agreeing to take a break if emotions run high. Active listening is also essential—focus on understanding your partner's perspective rather than planning your response. By approaching these conversations with empathy and patience, you create a supportive environment that allows you to express concerns and find solutions together.

Financial stress is a reality for many couples, but it doesn't have to define your relationship. By identifying the sources of stress and developing strategies to manage it, you can reduce its impact and create a more peaceful financial life. From debt management to open communication, these tools empower you to face financial challenges with confidence and support. Remember, you're not alone in this—working together can make even the toughest financial situations feel a little lighter.

Investing in the Future: Planning for Long-term Security

When you think about investing, it might feel like stepping into a whole new world. But really, it's about setting the stage for your future security and dreams. Investments are tools that help your money grow over time, and understanding the basics is where it all begins. You have stocks, which are shares of ownership in a company. They can be risky but also offer high rewards. Then, there are bonds and loans you give to a company or government in exchange for regular interest payments. These tend to be more stable. Mutual funds pool money from many investors to buy a diversified basket of stocks and bonds, offering a balanced approach. Each type of investment has its role in building long-term wealth, acting like different players in a team, each contributing to the overall success.

Creating a personalized investment strategy means tailoring your approach to fit your comfort level with risk and financial goals. Start by assessing your risk tolerance. Are you the type who can stomach market fluctuations, or do you prefer a more steady, predictable return? Conducting a risk assessment exercise can clarify this. Imagine it like a self-discovery session where you figure out what level of risk you are comfortable taking. From there, consider how diversifying your portfolio can spread that risk. It's like not putting all your eggs in one basket—by investing in a mix of different assets, you reduce the impact of a poor-performing investment. This strategy aligns with your risk tolerance and positions you to adapt to changing market conditions.

Retirement might seem far off, but planning for it now ensures a comfortable future. Consider various retirement account options, like 401(k)s or IRAs, which offer tax advantages that can boost your savings. Decide on how much you can contribute regularly. Even small amounts can grow significantly over time, thanks to compound interest. Picture this as planting seeds today that will grow into a forest of financial security later. Discuss your retirement goals with your partner, such as when you want to retire and what lifestyle you envision. This clarity helps determine how aggressively you need to save and invest. By planning together, you ensure that your retirement years are financially secure, fulfilling, and aligned with your shared vision.

Investments need attention and care, much like a garden that requires regular tending. This means regularly reviewing and adjusting your investment portfolio to align with your financial goals. Schedule annual investment review sessions to assess performance and make necessary adjustments. Some stocks have performed well and grown to take up too much of your portfolio, increasing your risk. You should rebalance by selling some of these and buying others to maintain your desired asset allocation. Consulting with financial advisors can provide expert guidance tailored to your situation, ensuring your investments remain on track. They offer insights into market trends and can help you navigate complex investment decisions. This ongoing evaluation keeps your investments healthy and poised for growth.

And just like that, our journey through financial harmony and planning draws close. From setting joint financial goals to investing in your future security, each step strengthens the foundation of your partnership. It's about more than just numbers; it's about aligning your resources with your shared dreams. As we move forward, let's explore how balancing individual and shared goals can further enrich your relationship.

CHAPTER 7

BALANCING INDIVIDUAL
AND SHARED GOALS

P icture a sunny afternoon at a local park, where you see a couple cheering each other on as they run side by side. They're training for a marathon, a goal they decided to pursue together despite having different paces. While one partner is faster and more experienced, the other is newer to running. Yet, their joint commitment to personal growth and shared experiences strengthens their bond. This story illustrates how supporting each other's ambitions can enhance a partnership, increasing satisfaction and fulfillment. Personal development isn't just about becoming the best version of yourself; it's about embracing your partner's journey, too. When you support each other's quests for growth, you create a relationship where both partners thrive, contributing to a dynamic and harmonious partnership.

Encouraging personal development involves more than just words of affirmation; it requires active participation in your partner's pursuits. Consider attending each other's significant events, like a book launch or an art exhibit. Your presence shows support and celebrates the milestones that mark their journey. Constructive feedback on personal projects can also be invaluable. Offering thoughtful insights or suggestions indicates your genuine interest and investment in their success. Remember, it's not about critiquing but sharing perspectives to help your partner grow. These actions demonstrate that you value their aspirations, contributing to a supportive and nurturing environment where both partners feel empowered to pursue their dreams.

Mutual encouragement transforms your relationship into a haven where each partner feels valued and inspired. When you cheer each other on, it creates a positive dynamic that fuels motivation and passion. Couples who practice this often find themselves thriving both individually and together. For instance, a couple who supports each other's career advancements may experience heightened relationship satisfaction as both partners feel understood and appreciated. This mutual encouragement also fosters resilience, providing a foundation to tackle challenges together. The joy of celebrating each other's achievements strengthens your emotional connection, reinforcing the idea that you are a team united in your journey toward growth and fulfillment.

Of course, supporting personal growth isn't without its challenges. Feelings of jealousy or competition can sometimes creep in, especially when one partner feels left behind. To navigate these obstacles, focus on open communication and honesty. Discuss any insecurities or concerns, and work together to find solutions that address these feelings. Remember, growth isn't a race; it's a shared experience where partners contribute to each other's success. By prioritizing transparency and empathy, you can maintain a healthy balance between individual ambitions and relationship harmony, paving the way for a partnership that flourishes with love and mutual respect.

Interactive Element: Growth Support Checklist

Objective: Strengthen your support for each other's personal growth.

Instructions:

1. **Identify Key Goals**: List each partner's individual goals and aspirations.
2. **Plan Supportive Actions**: Outline specific ways to support these goals, such as attending events, providing feedback, or offering resources.
3. **Schedule Regular Check-Ins**: Set aside time to discuss progress, challenges, and support needs.
4. **Celebrate Milestones**: Plan how to commemorate achievements, reinforcing mutual encouragement and satisfaction.

Setting and Achieving Couple's Goals

Setting shared goals as a couple is like charting a course for your relationship's future. It begins with identifying shared values and long-term visions. Imagine sitting down with a cup of coffee and discussing what truly matters to both of you. Is it building a home, traveling the world, or starting a family? You create a roadmap that guides your relationship forward by aligning your goals with these shared values. This process encourages you to dream together, fostering a sense of unity and purpose. It's about finding that sweet spot where both partners' aspirations converge, ensuring your goals are meaningful and motivating.

Once you've set your goals, tracking progress becomes key. Practical tools can make this process both fun and effective. Consider creating a couples' vision board. This visual representation of your goals is a daily reminder of what you're working towards. Hang it somewhere you both see often, like the living room or bedroom. A vision board isn't just a collection of images; it's a constant source of inspiration that keeps your goals front and center. Goal-setting apps tailored for partners can be significant for those who prefer digital tools. Apps like "Couple" or

"Raft" allow you to set milestones, track progress, and even send reminders. These tools help you stay organized and accountable, making it easier to achieve your shared objectives.

Compromise plays a significant role in achieving these goals. It's about finding a balance that respects both partners' needs and desires. Perhaps one partner wants to save for a dream vacation while the other is focused on paying off student loans. Negotiating timelines and priorities becomes crucial. This might mean delaying the vacation a little while you work on reducing debt. Flexibility and open communication are vital here. You ensure both partners feel heard and valued by approaching these discussions with empathy and understanding. This willingness to compromise strengthens your partnership, creating a relationship built on mutual respect and cooperation.

Celebrating milestones is an essential part of the goal-setting process. It reinforces success and keeps motivation high. Consider planning a special celebration or getaway when you hit a significant milestone. It doesn't have to be extravagant—a simple weekend trip or a special dinner can be enough to mark the occasion. Celebrations acknowledge the hard work you've put in and the progress you've made. They create joy and connection, reminding you why these goals matter. By taking time to celebrate, you enjoy the fruits of your labor and strengthen your bond, making your journey together all the more rewarding.

Balancing Career and Relationship Priorities

Balancing the demands of work and love can often feel like a tightrope. On one side, you have your career, with its deadlines, meetings, and ambitions. On the other hand, your relationship needs time, attention, and nurturing. The conflict between these two can create stress, especially when work responsibilities overshadow personal time. It's common to feel pulled in different directions, with time management issues adding to the chaos. You might find yourself checking emails during dinner or bringing work stress into your home life, leading to tension and burnout. Navigating these challenges requires intentional strategies to ensure that both areas of your life receive the attention they deserve.

Consider setting clear boundaries between work and personal time to manage this balance effectively. This might mean turning off work notifications after a particular hour or designating specific areas in your home as work-free zones. Another helpful practice is scheduling regular "work-free" evenings, where you both agree to put aside professional concerns and focus on each other. These evenings can be an opportunity to reconnect through a shared hobby, a simple dinner, or just a walk in the park. By creating these boundaries, you reinforce the importance of your relationship, ensuring that it remains a priority even amidst professional demands.

Open communication about career goals is crucial to maintaining harmony. Regular discussions about your aspirations help you understand how these goals impact your relationship. Whether considering a career change, a promotion, or furthering your education, sharing these thoughts with your partner is essential. Transparency fosters trust and ensures that both partners are on the same page. It also opens up a dialogue about supporting each other in achieving these goals. You can plan together by discussing potential challenges and opportunities, reducing surprises and misunderstandings.

When it comes to significant career decisions, joint decision-making is key. Evaluating relocation opportunities or job offers should be a collaborative process. Consider the impact on both your lives, discussing the pros and cons openly. This approach respects your partner's input and strengthens your bond as you navigate essential choices. It's about teamwork and recognizing that big decisions affect both of you. Working together ensures that your relationship remains supportive and integral to your professional journey.

Aligning Financial Goals for a Stronger Bond

Imagine two partners sitting at their kitchen table, discussing their dreams of buying a cozy home. They create a stable foundation for their relationship by setting shared financial goals. Financial alignment isn't just about dollars and cents; it's about reducing stress and enhancing harmony. When both partners agree on economic priorities, it eases tension and fosters a sense of teamwork. Consider how a couple that plans together to save for a vacation or a new car experiences less financial anxiety. This shared vision transforms potential points of conflict into opportunities for connection. Financial harmony becomes the bedrock upon which other aspects of the relationship can flourish, allowing you to focus on building a life together rather than worrying about monetary disagreements.

To achieve financial alignment, start by developing a joint budgeting plan. Sit together and outline your monthly income, expenses, and savings goals. This collaborative approach ensures that both partners are on the same page, understanding where money comes in and how it goes out. Next, set savings targets for future investments, whether a dream home, retirement, or a memorable trip. These targets provide motivation, turning abstract goals into tangible milestones. As you work together to meet these goals, you'll find a sense of accomplishment that strengthens your relationship. It's about taking control of your financial future and ensuring that your dreams are well within reach.

Managing joint finances effectively requires the right tools. Budgeting apps designed for couples, like Honeyfi or Goodbudget, can simplify this process. These apps help track spending, set budgets, and monitor progress, making financial management a shared responsibility. Consider attending financial planning workshops together. These sessions offer valuable insights into managing money wisely, providing strategies tailored to couples' needs. They also create a space for open dialogue about finances, encouraging a proactive approach to money management. These tools and resources empower you as a couple, turning financial planning from a chore into a collaborative adventure.

Financial conflicts can arise despite best efforts, often due to differing spending habits or priorities. To resolve these disagreements, focus on compromise. Discuss discretionary spending and saving priorities openly, finding a balance that respects both partners' needs. This might mean agreeing on a monthly budget for personal expenses while committing to a shared savings plan. By approaching these conversations with empathy and flexibility, you can navigate financial challenges without letting them disrupt your relationship. Remember, the goal is to build a partnership where financial decisions reflect mutual respect and shared aspirations.

Embracing Life Transitions Together

Life transitions can be like unexpected guests knocking on your door with little warning. Parenthood, relocation, and retirement are a few of these significant changes that impact relationships deeply. Each brings its own set of emotional and logistical challenges. Parenthood, for instance, can turn your world upside down with sleepless nights and an ever-growing list of responsibilities. Relocation might mean goodbye to familiar comforts and adjusting to a new environment. At the same time, retirement can shift daily routines and redefine roles within the relationship. These transitions, though daunting, are also opportunities for growth and bonding. They test your resilience as a couple and require you to adapt, communicate, and support each other in new ways.

Navigating these transitions as a team involves setting shared expectations and roles. It's about sitting down together and discussing what each transition means for both of you. For parenthood, this might involve deciding who takes on specific responsibilities with the baby or how household duties are divided. If you're relocating, talk about what you need to feel at home in a new place, whether finding a local community or setting up a cozy corner in your new house. Retirement might involve exploring new hobbies or deciding how to spend more time together. These conversations help ensure both partners feel valued and understood, creating a united front to face the changes.

Adaptability is key during life transitions. Being open-minded and flexible allows you to embrace changes without feeling overwhelmed. Practicing open communication about evolving needs is crucial. Your needs may shift as you adapt to new roles and situations. Discuss these changes openly, whether it's needing more emotional support or adjusting how you spend time together. This ongoing dialogue prevents misunderstandings and keeps you in sync. Embrace the idea that transitions are fluid, requiring you to adjust your sails as the winds change. By being adaptable, you not only navigate the transition more smoothly but also strengthen your relationship, knowing you can weather any storm together.

Creating rituals to honor transitions can also be a beautiful way to mark these significant changes. Consider hosting a "transition party" to celebrate a new phase, like moving into a new home or welcoming a baby. Invite friends and family to share in your joy and support. Alternatively, start a transition journal where you both document your thoughts, feelings, and experiences during this time. This practice provides a space for reflection and a tangible record of your journey together. Celebrating these transitions with intentionality adds meaning to the changes, transforming them from challenges into cherished memories. Through these rituals, you acknowledge the significance of each phase, honoring the past while looking forward to the future with hope and excitement.

Emotional Support: Being There for Each Other

When life throws curveballs, recognizing your partner's emotional needs becomes crucial. We all exhibit signs of stress differently. Some might retreat into silence, while others might become more irritable or anxious. Pay attention to these cues—changes in behavior, sleeping patterns, or even appetite can be telltale signs that something is amiss. Empathy and understanding are your allies here. They allow you to connect with your partner deeper, making them feel seen and heard. Approach these moments with gentle curiosity, asking open-ended questions like, "How are you feeling today?" or "Is there something on your mind?" Such inquiries invite your partner to share, creating a safe space for expression.

Consistent support is the backbone of emotional connection, especially during stressful times. Make it a habit to check in on each other regularly. These don't have to be long conversations; sometimes, a simple "How was your day?" can open the floodgates to meaningful dialogue. It's about being present, offering reassurance when needed, and comforting your partner with words or actions that say, "I'm here for you." This might mean sitting together in silence or offering a comforting touch. Such gestures reinforce your commitment to each other, nurturing the emotional bond that keeps your relationship strong.

Building resilience as a couple involves facing challenges together and transforming adversity into opportunities for growth. Engage in activities that strengthen your resilience as a team. This could be as simple as tackling a home project or participating in a new hobby together. Through these shared experiences, you learn to rely on each other, fostering trust and understanding. As you conquer obstacles, your relationship grows stronger, fortified by the challenges you've overcome together.

Creating a safe emotional space is vital for fostering openness and comfort. This means establishing non-judgmental communication practices where both partners feel secure in expressing their emotions. Set ground rules for these conversations, such as listening without interrupting or acknowledging each other's feelings without criticism. Encourage a culture of openness where vulnerability is welcomed and supported. When both partners feel safe to share, the relationship becomes a sanctuary of trust and love.

Spiritual Anchors: Finding Strength in Faith

When life throws unexpected challenges your way, leaning on spiritual beliefs can offer a comforting refuge. Faith provides stability and hope, acting as a guiding light in difficult times. Consider the powerful words of Psalm 46:1, "God is our refuge and strength, a very present help in trouble." Such passages remind you that you are not alone, instilling courage and offering peace amidst turmoil. These verses become lifelines, grounding you when everything else seems uncertain. As you reflect on these scriptures, let them reassure you that faith can be a steadfast anchor, offering solace and direction when needed.

Incorporating prayer and meditation into your daily routine is another way to find peace and clarity. During crises, developing a specific prayer routine can be particularly helpful. Set aside a few moments daily to express your fears, hopes, and gratitude through prayer. This practice can be a source of comfort, a moment to pause and reconnect with your inner self and each other. Guided meditation also serves as an excellent tool for stress relief. By focusing on your breath and letting go of tension, you can achieve a sense of calm and perspective. These practices help clear your mind, allowing you to approach challenges with renewed strength and clarity.

Seeking community support is invaluable when navigating challenging times. Your faith community can provide a network of understanding and empathy, offering encouragement and shared wisdom. Participating in faith-based support groups can be a source of strength, where you can share experiences and draw on collective beliefs and values. This sense of community reinforces that you are part of something larger, providing reassurance and comfort. It reminds you that others have walked similar paths and that a network of love and faith supports you. Engaging with this community can be a powerful way to bolster your spiritual resilience.

Crises also present opportunities for spiritual reflection and growth. You can gain insights into your spiritual journey by journaling your thoughts and feelings. Use prompts like, "What has this experience taught me about faith?" or "How has my relationship with God changed during this time?" These reflections can help you process emotions and recognize the spiritual milestones you've achieved through adversity. Celebrate these achievements, acknowledging the growth and strength that have emerged from difficult times. Through reflection, you can transform challenges into catalysts for spiritual development, enriching your faith and deepening your connection to each other.

Navigating Health Challenges: Supporting Wellness Together

Facing a health crisis can feel like navigating uncharted waters. Whether it's managing a chronic illness or addressing mental health concerns, the journey can be daunting. Chronic illnesses often require ongoing care and adjustments to daily life. They can impact everything from your routine to your emotional well-being. Mental health issues, though sometimes less visible, can be equally challenging. They demand awareness, understanding, and proactive management. Recognizing the signs early and taking proactive steps can make a significant difference. It's about being prepared, knowing the potential hurdles, and working together to overcome them. When both partners are committed to health management, they can create a supportive environment that fosters healing and resilience.

Creating a health support plan is a vital step in managing these challenges. Begin by sitting down together to outline roles and responsibilities. Who will handle medical appointments and treatments? Will one partner be more involved in coordinating medication schedules? Establishing a routine for medication and care is crucial. It ensures consistency and reduces the risk of missed doses or appointments. Consider using a shared calendar to keep track of appointments and medication times. This helps stay organized and reinforces the idea that you're a team working together to tackle the challenges ahead. By clearly defining roles, you can alleviate stress and ensure that both partners feel supported and involved.

Maintaining emotional and physical well-being requires a holistic approach. Start by incorporating stress-reduction techniques into your daily routine. This could be as simple as practicing deep breathing exercises or engaging in yoga. Encourage each other to stay active, whether a daily walk or a workout session at the gym. Physical activity not only boosts health but also lifts spirits. Alongside exercise, focus on healthy eating habits. Cooking together can be fun for exploring nutritious meals, turning a necessity into a shared experience. By prioritizing these aspects of wellness, you create a foundation that supports both your body and mind, providing the strength needed to face health challenges.

Open communication about health concerns is essential. It's about creating a safe space where both partners can express worries, fears, and needs without judgment. Use active listening techniques to ensure understanding and empathy. Sometimes, just being heard can make all the difference. These conversations build trust and reinforce your commitment to each other's well-being. When both partners feel comfortable discussing health issues openly, it fosters a partnership where challenges are faced together, not alone.

Navigating health challenges requires teamwork, understanding, and open communication. It's about creating a supportive environment where both partners feel valued, heard, and empowered to face whatever comes their way. As you continue this journey together, remember that each step you take strengthens your bond and reinforces your commitment to each other's well-being. In the next chapter, we'll explore the power of creating a positive and supportive environment, focusing on building a home that nurtures love and growth.

CHAPTER 8

CREATING A POSITIVE AND SUPPORTIVE ENVIRONMENT

I magine coming home after a long day; you feel a sense of peace when you step through the door. It's not just a physical space you're entering; it's a sanctuary that nurtures your relationship and your well-being. Your home should be a retreat from the chaos of the outside world, a place where you can relax, recharge, and connect with your partner. By redefining your home environment, you can cultivate a sense of calm and tranquility that supports your emotional and mental health.

Start by considering the power of simplicity. Decluttering your space can have a profound effect on your mindset and mood. When you remove excess items, you create a calming atmosphere that invites relaxation and focus. Studies have shown that clutter can prevent positive energy flow, keeping you overwhelmed (SOURCE 1). Take a weekend to review your belongings, keeping only what truly serves you and brings joy. As you clear physical clutter, you'll find that your mind feels more precise, too, making room for peace and contentment.

Incorporating colors and lighting that promote relaxation can further enhance this serene environment. Soft, muted tones like pale blues, greens, and earthy neutrals can create a soothing backdrop for your home. These colors have been shown to reduce stress and promote a sense of calm (SOURCE 1). Complement these hues with lighting miming natural sunlight, using lamps and fixtures that cast a warm, inviting glow. This combination of color and light can transform your home into a sanctuary that nurtures your spirit.

Nature has an incredible ability to soothe and heal, so consider bringing elements of the outdoors inside. Indoor plants can purify the air, boost your mood, and add a touch of natural beauty to your space. Choose varieties that are easy to care for, like snake plants or pothos, and place them strategically around your home to create a sense of harmony. Natural decor, such as wooden accents or stone features, can also enhance the feeling of serenity. If you have outdoor space, turn it into a peaceful retreat with comfortable seating, soft lighting, and lush greenery. This outdoor sanctuary can be perfect for morning coffee, evening reflections, or simply enjoying each other's company.

Designing spaces within your home that facilitate connection and communication is essential for nurturing your relationship. Create cozy nooks where you can have intimate conversations, free from distractions. A comfortable chair by the window, a loveseat tucked into a quiet corner, or even a window seat with plush cushions can become the perfect spot for meaningful talks. These spaces invite you to slow down and connect, fostering a deeper understanding and appreciation of each other.

Open-layout dining areas can encourage shared meals and conversations. Arrange your dining space to invite interaction with a round table that allows for easy eye contact and engagement. Make mealtimes a priority, setting aside devices and distractions to focus on each other. These moments of togetherness can strengthen your bond, providing opportunities to share stories, laugh, and discuss the day's events. By creating spaces that prioritize connection, you reinforce your commitment to nurturing your relationship.

Maintaining a tranquil environment amidst life's chaos requires intentionality and effort. Establish quiet hours in your home, times when you can unplug from technology and the outside world's noise. Use this time for relaxation, reflection, or simply being present with each other. Implement noise-reduction techniques, such as using curtains, rugs, or soft furnishings to absorb sound and create a peaceful atmosphere. By cultivating a home that supports tranquility, you develop a foundation of peace that sustains you through the ups and downs of daily life.

Interactive Element: Home Sanctuary Checklist

Objective: Transform your home into a sanctuary of peace and connection.

Instructions:

1. **Declutter**: Spend a day clearing out items that no longer serve you. Donate, recycle, or repurpose anything that clutters your space and mind.
2. **Choose Calming Colors**: Select paint or decor in soothing tones like blues and greens. Incorporate these colors into your walls, textiles, and accessories.
3. **Incorporate Natural Elements**: Add plants and natural decor, such as wood or stone, to create a sense of harmony.
4. **Create Connection Spaces**: Designate areas for intimate conversations and shared meals. Arrange furniture to encourage engagement and interaction.
5. **Establish Quiet Hours**: Set times each day for unplugging and winding down. Use these moments for relaxation and connection.

By following these steps, you can create a home environment that nurtures your relationship and enriches your personal well-being.

Though simple, these changes can profoundly impact your daily life, fostering a sense of peace and support that enhances your bond and strengthens your connection.

Spiritual Alignment: Harmonizing Beliefs and Practices

Creating a shared spiritual vision is like painting a picture of the life you both envision, using broad strokes of faith and shared values. Picture yourselves sitting down together, discussing what truly matters in your spiritual lives. It's not just about agreeing on everything but finding those common threads that weave your beliefs into a cohesive tapestry. Begin with a joint vision statement exercise. This involves writing down what you both want your spiritual life to look like. It could be about being more involved in your community or deepening your faith practices. This statement is a compass guiding you toward a shared spiritual destination. Identifying shared spiritual goals is the next step. These could be goals like attending a retreat together, committing to volunteer work, or dedicating more time to family prayer. Whatever they are, they should reflect your collective aspirations and provide a roadmap for your spiritual journey together.

Consistent spiritual practices are crucial to keeping your shared vision alive and thriving. Daily or weekly routines, like family devotionals, can be an excellent way to bring everyone together. Choose a time that works for everyone: Sunday evenings or a quiet morning mid-week. These moments become anchors in your routine, creating a rhythm that keeps your spiritual connection strong. Also, consider monthly spiritual retreats or reflection days. These don't have to be elaborate getaways; they can be simple afternoons spent in nature or quiet evenings with a good book and some reflective conversation. The key is setting aside time for spiritual renewal, allowing you to reconnect with each other and your faith.

Celebrating spiritual milestones is integral to honoring your journey as a couple. These milestones could be anything from the anniversary of a significant spiritual event, like a baptism or a commitment ceremony, to personal achievements in your faith. By commemorating these moments, you acknowledge your growth and progress together. Consider hosting small gatherings with friends who share your spiritual journey. These gatherings can be informal, a simple meal, or an evening of shared stories and laughter. They provide an opportunity to reflect on where you've been and where you're going, reinforcing the bonds that tie you together.

Encouraging spiritual dialogue is essential for maintaining a healthy and evolving spiritual relationship. Set aside time for monthly spiritual check-ins, where you both can talk openly about your beliefs, doubts, and discoveries. These discussions should be judgment-free, creating a space where both partners feel heard and respected. It's a time to share what's on your heart, to ask questions, and to explore new ideas together. Creating a shared spiritual reading list can also be a fantastic way to foster dialogue. Choose books or articles that interest you both and take turns reading them. Then, discuss your thoughts and insights, allowing the material to spark deeper conversations about your beliefs and how they shape your lives.

Spiritual alignment is not about losing individuality but creating a harmonious blend of your unique beliefs and practices. It's an ongoing process that requires patience, understanding, and a willingness to grow together. As you explore these practices, your spiritual life becomes more prosperous and fulfilling, providing a solid foundation for your relationship. This chapter is about finding that balance, where both partners feel supported and valued and where your spiritual lives enhance your bond meaningfully.

Encouraging Creativity: Expressing Love through Actions

Think back to the last time you did something creative for your partner. It could be a simple handwritten note tucked into their lunch bag or a playlist you curated just for them. These gestures, though small, carry tremendous weight. They speak the language of love in ways that words sometimes can't. When you take the time to create something with your own hands or put thought into a personalized gift, you express appreciation and affection in a uniquely intimate manner. Homemade gifts or crafts, for instance, are not just objects; they are embodiments of your care and effort. Whether it's a scrapbook filled with cherished memories or a hand-knitted scarf inspired by their favorite color, these creations hold a special place in both your hearts. Personalized playlists or artwork can also weave a narrative of your shared experiences, offering a tangible reminder of the bond you cherish. Imagine the joy of receiving a playlist that perfectly captures the soundtrack of your relationship, each song a chapter in your love story. These creative expressions convey love and deepen your connection, reflecting the time and thought invested in celebrating your partner's uniqueness.

Consider setting up a dedicated space in your home to foster an environment that encourages creativity. This doesn't have to be a grand studio; even a tiny corner with a table and some supplies can spark inspiration. Stock it with materials you both enjoy—paints, sketchbooks, fabric, or even a simple journal. This space becomes a haven for spontaneous creative projects, where you can retreat whenever inspiration strikes. Encourage each other to explore these projects without the pressure of perfection. The goal is to enjoy the process and the time spent together, not just the final product. By nurturing a creative atmosphere, you invite playfulness and imagination into your relationship, fostering a sense of wonder and discovery that strengthens your bond.

Engaging in creative activities can be a delightful way to nurture your relationship and your individual talents. For example, cooking new recipes as a team can turn an ordinary evening into an adventure of flavors and teamwork. Choose a dish you've never tried before and dive into the experience together, from shopping for ingredients to savoring the final creation. The kitchen becomes your playground, where creativity and collaboration blend seamlessly. Attending art classes or workshops can offer new perspectives and skills, whether pottery, painting, or photography. These shared experiences expand your horizons and create lasting memories as you learn and grow alongside each other. By immersing yourselves in creative pursuits, you cultivate a shared sense of accomplishment and joy, enriching your relationship with each new endeavor.

Recognizing and valuing each partner's creative contributions is crucial in maintaining a supportive and loving partnership. Displaying each other's artwork or projects at home can be an excellent way to celebrate your talents. Whether it's hanging a painting in the living room or showcasing a handmade quilt on the bed, these displays become daily reminders of your support and admiration. They also invite conversations and compliments from guests, further validating your creative efforts. Creating a shared creativity journal can be another meaningful way to document ideas and inspirations. Use this journal as a repository for sketches, notes, and plans for future projects. It becomes a collaborative canvas where you contribute to a growing tapestry of creativity. This practice honors your individual expressions and reinforces the importance of creativity in your relationship, encouraging both partners to continue exploring and sharing their gifts.

Let creativity be a bridge that connects you, a path that leads to deeper understanding and appreciation. The love you express through creative acts becomes a testament to your commitment and care, a tapestry woven with the threads of imagination and heart. As you explore these creative pathways, you may discover new facets of each other and your relationship, enriching the bond that ties you together.

The Power of Rituals: Building Meaningful Traditions

Rituals and traditions are like the glue that holds relationships together, providing stability and a sense of shared identity. They carve out moments of connection in the ebb and flow of daily life, grounding you in the things that truly matter. Research shows that rituals significantly impact relationship satisfaction by creating predictable patterns and moments of togetherness. They help couples stay connected, especially during busy or challenging times, by offering familiar anchors to return to. Think about it— what are the rituals that define your relationship? Maybe it's that Sunday morning coffee, where you both sit down, mugs in hand, and talk about your week. Or perhaps it's how you celebrate each anniversary with a special dinner or revisit a place that holds fond memories. These rituals give your relationship a rhythm, a heartbeat that pulses with love and continuity. They serve as reminders of the bond you share, offering comfort and a sense of belonging.

Developing personalized couple rituals is an opportunity to uniquely reflect your values and relationship dynamics. Consider what matters most to you both—what activities or traditions bring you joy and connection? Maybe it's a Sunday morning coffee and reflection time, where you set aside an hour to catch up on life, discuss dreams, and share gratitude for each other. This simple ritual can become a cherished tradition, a time when nothing else matters but the two of you. Anniversary rituals and celebrations are another chance to create meaningful traditions. Perhaps you write letters to each other every year, capturing memories, hopes, and dreams for the future. Or you might plan a getaway, revisiting places that have played a significant role in your journey together. These personalized rituals become touchstones that remind you of your love story, reinforcing your commitment and affection.

Blending family traditions and creating new ones enriches your relationship by honoring both partners' backgrounds. When two lives come together, so do two sets of traditions, and finding ways to integrate these can be a rewarding experience. Holiday rituals that honor both partners' backgrounds can be a beautiful expression of unity. You could combine a traditional Christmas dinner with a Hanukkah celebration or create a new Thanksgiving tradition that incorporates elements from both cultures. These blended traditions celebrate your individual heritages and create a unique family culture that reflects your shared values. Annual family reunions or gatherings can be another meaningful tradition. Hosting an event where both families come together fosters a sense of community and belonging, allowing everyone to share in the joy of your relationship. These gatherings become a time to connect, reminisce, and create new memories, strengthening the bonds between you and your partner and your wider family circle.

Keeping rituals alive and evolving is essential as your relationship grows and changes. Seasonal or life-stage adjustments to rituals can ensure they remain relevant and meaningful. As life changes— perhaps with the arrival of children or a move to a new city—your rituals may need to adapt to fit your new circumstances. Involving future generations in family traditions can be an excellent way to pass on the values and love that define your relationship. Whether teaching your children the art of making grandma's famous cookies or sharing stories of family traditions during the holidays, these moments create a lineage of love and connection that spans generations. They become a legacy, a way of keeping your shared history alive and thriving.

Rituals are not just about repeating the same actions; they're about creating a tapestry of shared experiences that weave together the fabric of your love. They provide a framework that supports your relationship, offering comfort and continuity amidst life's ever-changing landscape. Whether grand or simple, these rituals become the stories you tell, the memories you cherish, and the foundation upon which your relationship stands. As you explore and develop these traditions, you'll find that they offer stability, joy, and celebration, enhancing the depth and richness of your connection. These practices ensure that your love, like a well-tended garden, continues to grow and flourish, rooted in the shared values and experiences that define your unique journey together.

CHAPTER 9

SUSTAINING LONG-TERM RELATIONSHIP HEALTH

Picture this: you and your partner sit together on a quiet Sunday afternoon, sipping coffee and reflecting on your journey together. Looking back, you realize how much you've grown, how many challenges you've overcome, and how many dreams you've built. This moment of reflection isn't just a pleasant trip down memory lane. It's a vital practice, a relationship check-up that ensures you're both on the same path and aligned with your goals. Regular check-ups are like tune-ups for your relationship, helping you stay connected and satisfied as you navigate life's ups and downs.

Scheduling bi-annual relationship assessments can be a game-changer. Think of it as setting aside time twice yearly to focus solely on your relationship. These assessments are not just about identifying what's not working but celebrating what is. They provide an opportunity to acknowledge your successes, learn from your challenges, and set new intentions for the future. During these check-ups, you can discuss any changes in your goals or circumstances, ensuring you're both on the same page. Making these assessments a routine creates a space for growth, understanding, and renewed commitment.

A structured framework is needed to make these check-ups effective. You can start with self-assessment questionnaires that explore different aspects of your relationship, from communication and emotional intimacy to shared activities and goals. These questionnaires clearly show where you stand and where you want to focus your efforts. Analyzing your communication patterns, for example, can reveal areas that need improvement and highlight strengths you might not have recognized. By closely examining these elements, you can identify patterns and make informed decisions about enhancing your relationship.

Addressing areas for improvement is a crucial part of the process. Once you've identified the aspects that need attention, it's time to create action plans. This is where setting SMART goals comes into play. SMART goals are Specific, Measurable, Achievable, Relevant, and Time-bound, providing a clear roadmap for improvement. For instance, if you want to enhance your communication, a SMART goal might be to set aside fifteen minutes each evening to discuss your day. You can make meaningful progress and strengthen your connection by focusing on achievable steps.

Reaffirming shared goals is another key component of these check-ups. As life evolves, so do your priorities and aspirations. Taking the time to revisit and adjust your goals ensures they reflect your current values and circumstances. Consider organizing joint goal-setting retreats where you can dream, plan, and strategize together. These retreats offer a chance to reconnect with your shared vision and reignite the passion that brought you together in the first place. You create a united front by aligning your goals, ready to tackle whatever life throws your way.

Interactive Element: Relationship Check-Up Exercise

1. **Schedule a Date**: Choose a time twice yearly for your

relationship check-up. Mark it on your calendar as a non-negotiable date.

2. **Prepare Your Questions**: Create a list of self-assessment questions covering communication, intimacy, and shared goals.

3. **Reflect and Discuss**: Answer the questions individually, then share your responses. Discuss insights and areas for improvement.

4. **Set SMART Goals**: Identify one or two areas to focus on and set SMART goals to guide your efforts.

5. **Plan a Retreat**: Organize a mini-retreat to revisit and reaffirm your shared goals. Use this time to dream, plan, and reconnect.

Embracing Change: Adapting to Life's Seasons

Change, as inevitable as the tides, is a constant in life and relationships. When you think you've got everything figured out, life throws you a curveball—whether it's a new job, a move across the country, or even the arrival of a child. Recognizing the signs of impending change can sometimes be subtle. Maybe it's a feeling of restlessness or the sense that something new is on the horizon. These are the moments when adaptability becomes your greatest ally. Embracing change rather than resisting it can be the key to maintaining a healthy, thriving relationship. It requires a willingness to evolve and an openness to life's unexpected paths.

Cultivating a flexible mindset is essential in navigating these shifts. Flexibility doesn't mean you abandon your values or goals; instead, it means you're open to adjusting your approach as circumstances change. Practicing mindfulness can be an effective way to reduce resistance to change. By staying present and aware, you can better manage anxiety and face new situations calmly and clearly. Mindfulness helps you acknowledge your feelings about change without being overwhelmed by them. It's like finding a still point in the chaos, allowing you to respond thoughtfully rather than impulsively. Encouraging open-minded discussions with your partner also plays a crucial role. These conversations should be safe spaces where you feel comfortable expressing fears, hopes, and ideas about the changes ahead. By approaching discussions with curiosity and empathy, you create a supportive environment for exploring new possibilities together.

When major life transitions occur, navigating them as a united front is vital. This means creating a transition support plan that outlines how you'll manage the changes together. Start by identifying the specific challenges you might face and brainstorm solutions collaboratively. Whether dividing responsibilities, setting new routines, or seeking external support, having a plan can provide stability amidst uncertainty. Additionally, recognize that transitions are not just logistical but emotional journeys. Being there for each other and offering reassurance and encouragement can make the difference between feeling overwhelmed and empowered.

Sharing personal growth experiences during times of change can significantly strengthen your relationship. As you face new challenges, you'll likely find yourselves growing in unexpected ways. You may discover new strengths or better understand each other's needs and perspectives. Sharing these experiences openly can deepen your connection and reinforce the trust and intimacy you've built. It's about recognizing that change, while sometimes challenging, can also bring opportunities for growth and closeness. Embracing change together is not just about surviving life's seasons; it's about thriving through them, hand in hand, ready to face whatever comes next with resilience and love.

Celebrating Milestones: Acknowledging Growth Together

In the hustle and bustle of daily life, it's easy to let the days blur together, missing the significance of the moments that mark your relationship's progress. Milestones are those shining points that remind you of how far you've come and how much you've accomplished together. Historically, milestone celebrations have been used to mark rites of passage, achievements, and transitions, serving as a pause to reflect and appreciate. In relationships, they play a similar role. Whether it's your first anniversary, the day you moved into your first home, or the celebration of a shared achievement, these moments deserve acknowledgment. They offer a chance to step back and recognize the growth, resilience, and love that have brought you to this point. Each milestone is a testament to your shared journey, a reminder of the challenges overcome and the dreams realized.

Planning meaningful celebrations isn't about extravagance; it's about creating memories that resonate with your story. Consider an anniversary getaway or a simple staycation where you can disconnect from the world and reconnect with each other. Choose a place that holds significance—perhaps where you had your first date or a location that has always been on your bucket list. If travel isn't feasible, create a timeline of your relationship's significant moments. Use photos, memorabilia, or a digital slideshow to revisit your shared laughs, tears, and smiles. This timeline can serve as a visual reminder of your shared history, sparking conversations and reflections on your journey together. It's about creating a space where you can bask in the glow of your accomplishments, both big and small.

Incorporating rituals of gratitude into these celebrations can deepen the experience. Take a moment to write each other love letters or gratitude notes, expressing appreciation for the qualities and moments that make your relationship unique. These letters can be shared during your celebration as heartfelt reminders of your love and commitment. Gratitude amplifies joy, reinforcing the bond you share by focusing on the positive aspects of your partnership. It's a practice that enriches your celebrations and leaves a lasting impact, encouraging ongoing appreciation and affection. By consciously acknowledging what you cherish about each other, you create a reservoir of positive memories that can be drawn upon during challenging times.

Documenting these milestone memories ensures they remain a part of your shared narrative. Consider creating a scrapbook or digital album filled with photos, notes, and mementos from your celebrations. This tangible collection can be revisited whenever you need a reminder of the love and growth you've experienced together. It's a keepsake that captures the essence of your celebrations and serves as inspiration for future milestones. Looking back on these memories can reignite the spark, offering a sense of continuity and perspective. It's a way of honoring your journey, celebrating where you've been, and looking forward to what lies ahead. As you continue to grow together, these documented memories will serve as a testament to the love and dedication that define your relationship.

Continuous Learning: Growing Together Through Life

Imagine the thrill of discovering something new, not alone, but with your partner by your side. Continuous learning as a couple is like embarking on an endless adventure, where each new skill or knowledge enhances your shared world. It's about embracing curiosity and making personal development a cornerstone of your relationship. Couples who commit to learning together often find that it enriches their lives and strengthens their bond. Whether attending workshops, seminars, or exploring hobbies you've always been curious about, learning together opens doors to new experiences and perspectives. Picture yourselves taking a weekend cooking class or attending a seminar on a topic neither of you know much about. These shared experiences can spark conversations, laughter, and a deeper connection as you both navigate unfamiliar territory hand in hand.

But learning isn't just about formal education; it's about recognizing that your partner is a treasure trove of knowledge. Every day, there's something new to learn from each other. Your partner may be a whiz at gardening while you've got a knack for fixing things around the house. Share those skills. It's in these exchanges that you find inspiration and growth. Why not start by exchanging book recommendations? Maybe there's a novel that moved you or a self-help book that gave you a fresh perspective. These shared insights illuminate each other's minds and hearts, fostering understanding and empathy. As you explore these new worlds, your conversations deepen, strengthening your bond.

Setting learning goals as a couple is another way to ensure you're both growing in ways that matter to you. It's not about strict objectives but setting intentions that align with your interests and aspirations. You can learn a new language or take a painting class. Setting these goals together turns them into shared adventures. Plan how you'll tackle these goals, whether signing up for a weekly class or dedicating an hour each weekend to practice. These goals create a sense of purpose and direction, offering you something to look forward to and work towards.

Reflecting on your learning experiences is just as important as the learning itself. Make it a habit to hold monthly review sessions where you both discuss what you've learned, how it's impacted you, and what you'd like to explore next. These sessions can be casual, over dinner, or during a walk in the park. The idea is to celebrate achievements and insights, no matter how small. You could have finally mastered that recipe or finished a challenging book. Recognize these milestones and discuss how they've enriched your lives. This reflection affirms your progress and sets the stage for future learning experiences, keeping the growth cycle vibrant and ongoing.

Building a Legacy: Leaving a Lasting Impact

When you think about the legacy you want to leave behind, it's not just about tangible things like money or possessions. It's about the

94

values, the love, and the impact you've had on those around you. Together with your partner, you have the opportunity to define what that legacy will look like. It starts with a legacy vision statement. This is a powerful exercise where you and your partner sit down and articulate the core values and contributions you wish to be remembered for. Are kindness and generosity at the top of your list? Or creativity and perseverance? Whatever it is, writing it down makes it real. It serves as a guiding light, helping you make decisions that align with the legacy you want to create. This simple exercise can transform abstract ideas into a concrete path forward, giving you a sense of purpose and direction.

Contributing positively to your community is a significant part of building that legacy. Think about the causes that resonate with you both. Is it environmental conservation, education, or supporting the arts? Volunteering for local charities can be an enriching way to give back and make a difference. It's not just about the time you give; it's about the connections you make and the hope you inspire. Hosting community events or fundraisers can also amplify your impact. Imagine organizing a charity run or a bake sale, rallying your neighbors around a common cause. These activities don't just benefit the community; they strengthen your bond as a couple as you work together to bring about positive change. By contributing to your community, you weave yourselves into its fabric, leaving a legacy of compassion and care.

Nurturing future generations is another cornerstone of a lasting legacy. Whether you have children, grandchildren, or young people in your life, you hold the power to shape their futures. Establishing family traditions can provide a sense of identity and continuity, passing down values and wisdom. It could be a Sunday dinner tradition where everyone shares a week's highlight or an annual trip to a place with family significance. Writing a family history or memoir can also be a priceless gift. Capturing your stories, lessons, and experiences ensures your legacy lives on, guiding those who come after you. It's a way to share the richness of your life and the wisdom you've gained, creating a lasting impact on those who read it. By nurturing future generations, you invest in a legacy that extends beyond your lifetime, touching the lives of those who follow.

Celebrating the ongoing journey of building a legacy is as important as the acts themselves. It's about taking a moment to reflect on what you've achieved and the difference you've made. Organize annual legacy reflection and celebration gatherings. Invite family and friends to join you in honoring the progress you've made and the goals you've set. These gatherings can be a time to share stories, express gratitude, and reignite your commitment to making a positive impact. They remind you of the values you hold dear and the legacy you're building. In these moments, you celebrate what you've accomplished and reinforce your dedication to your shared vision. As you celebrate, you inspire those around you to consider their legacies, creating positive change. Building a legacy isn't a one-time effort; it's an ongoing journey of love, growth, and contribution. By embracing this journey, you and your partner create a rich life with meaning and impact.

CHAPTER 10

OVERCOMING OBJECTIONS AND CHALLENGES

Imagine standing in the middle of a bustling city street, the noise of life swirling around you like a relentless storm. You're juggling a demanding job, chasing after kids, and trying to keep up with the endless chores that never seem to stop. Finding time for devotionals is like searching for a needle in a haystack. You're certainly not alone in this struggle. Many couples face similar challenges, trying to carve out even a tiny moment for spiritual connection amidst the chaos. But what if I told you that making time for devotionals could be like finding a calm oasis in the middle of your busy life?

One of the most common constraints is the demanding work schedules that often interrupt our time. Many of you might find your days packed from morning to night, leaving little room for anything else. Add to that the parenting and family commitments that fill any remaining gaps in your schedule, and you're left wondering how to start incorporating devotionals. The good news is there are ways to work around these hurdles. It's about finding those little pockets of time and making them count. You might not have an hour to spare, but five minutes can be as powerful when used intentionally.

Consider the strategy of time-blocking for spiritual activities. This technique involves setting aside specific blocks of time in your schedule dedicated solely to devotionals. It might be as simple as reserving ten minutes during your lunch break or setting a consistent time before bed. Integrating devotionals into existing routines can also make a big difference. Think about those moments when you're already in a routine, like your morning coffee or evening wind-down. These can become opportunities for a quick devotional, seamlessly fitting into your day without adding extra pressure.

Quick and impactful devotional practices can transform how you experience spirituality in your busy lifestyle. You don't need to spend hours in meditation to feel the benefits. Two-minute gratitude reflections or scripture meditation during your daily commute can bring peace and mindfulness to even the most hectic day. These brief moments of reflection can act as spiritual resets, helping you center yourself and focus on what truly matters. It's about quality, not quantity. And those small, consistent efforts can add to significant change over time.

Prioritizing devotionals can have profound benefits for both personal and relational well-being. Engaging in these practices regularly can reduce stress and promote mindfulness, allowing you to approach life's challenges with a calmer mindset. You'll find that these moments of spiritual connection can strengthen your bond with your partner, providing a shared sense of purpose and understanding. It's like creating a sanctuary within your relationship where you feel supported and connected. By prioritizing devotionals, you're investing in yourselves and each other, fostering a deeper, more meaningful connection.

Interactive Element: Quick Devotional Planner

Take a moment to map out your week with a Quick Devotional Planner. Identify three short time slots where you can incorporate devotionals, such as during your morning routine, lunch break, or before bed. To fill those slots, write down specific practices, like a gratitude reflection or scripture reading. Keep this planner visible to remind you of these moments, and adjust as needed to fit your schedule. This small step can help you stay committed and find those precious moments of peace amidst your busy life.

Customizing Devotionals for Unique Relationship Needs

Every relationship has rhythm and intricacies, like a pair of dancers finding their steps together. Identifying your specific devotional needs starts with recognizing the unique spiritual maturity levels each of you brings. One partner may be deeply rooted in their faith, while the other is beginning to explore spiritual avenues. This diversity can enrich your devotional practice if approached with curiosity and openness. It's also important to consider how you prefer to learn and interact. Some people absorb information best through reading, while others might find that listening to a podcast resonates more. Understanding these preferences allows you to tailor your devotionals in a natural and engaging way for both of you.

To personalize your devotional content, select themes that align with your personal experiences and current life situations. Devotionals focusing on trust and courage might be particularly meaningful if you're navigating a season of change. You could also create personalized reflection questions that dive deeper into themes that resonate with both of you. These questions can prompt thoughtful discussions, helping you connect more deeply. For example, after reading a devotional about gratitude, you might ask, "What are three things in our relationship that you're grateful for today?" This simple question can open the door to heartfelt conversations and a renewed appreciation for each other.

Flexibility is key to keeping your devotionals fresh and engaging. You can prevent the practice from becoming stagnant by rotating formats and mediums. One week, you might focus on written devotionals. At the same time, the next, you could switch to listening to a spiritually enriching podcast together during a drive. Incorporating multimedia resources like videos or audiobooks can also add variety and depth, catering to different learning styles and keeping both partners interested. This adaptability ensures that your devotional time remains a source of inspiration and connection rather than becoming another item on the to-do list.

The impact can be profound when devotionals are tailored to your relationship's unique needs. You'll likely notice increased enthusiasm for spiritual activities as each partner feels the practice speaks to their journey. This personalized approach fosters deeper mutual insights as you explore relevant and meaningful themes. Engaging in devotionals that truly resonate can lead to significant spiritual growth, both individually and as a couple. It's about creating a spiritual environment where both partners feel seen, heard, and valued, allowing your relationship to flourish in faith.

Engaging with devotionals in this personalized way can transform your spiritual practice into a cherished ritual. As you continue to explore and adapt your approach, you'll likely find new ways to connect and your faith. This dynamic Process strengthens your relationship and enriches your spiritual lives, offering a shared path of growth and discovery.

Engaging a Reluctant Partner

Picture a quiet evening at home. You're eager to share a moment of peace with your partner through a devotional. Yet, you notice their hesitation. It's a common scenario. Sometimes, reluctance stems from past negative experiences. Perhaps they've attended a service that felt judgmental or participated in a less-than-welcoming group. These memories can create a barrier to trying again. Other times, it might be a perceived lack of time or relevance. With busy lives and the constant pressure to stay productive, it's easy to see devotionals as an extra task rather than a source of peace. For some, the idea doesn't fit into their vision of what's essential. Understanding these reasons is the first step in addressing them with compassion.

Encouraging your partner to join you in devotionals requires a gentle touch. Start by inviting them casually, without any pressure. An invitation to sit with a warm cup of tea and a short passage can feel more like a shared moment than a structured activity. Sharing your benefits and experiences can also be a powerful motivator. Explain how these moments have brought you clarity or peace. Let them see your positive changes, and it might spark curiosity. Your enthusiasm can be contagious, but it's crucial to approach the topic with empathy and respect for their feelings.

Patience and understanding are your greatest allies in this endeavor. Allowing space for personal reflection is key. Your partner might need time to process their feelings about devotionals before they're ready to participate. It's important to respect their spiritual journey, acknowledging everyone's path is unique. Please encourage them to explore at their own pace. This respect can open doors to discussions that might otherwise remain closed. It's about creating an environment where both partners feel comfortable expressing their thoughts and feelings, fostering mutual growth without pressure.

The benefits of shared devotionals extend beyond just a spiritual connection. Participating together can improve communication and empathy. As you discuss the themes and passages, you'll learn more about each other's perspectives and values. This exchange deepens your understanding and appreciation of one another. It's like peeling back layers to reveal the core of who you are, and it strengthens your foundation. Moreover, a shared spiritual practice can enhance your relationship, providing a common ground that reinforces your bond. You're building a spiritual foundation that supports your relationship, offering stability and unity amidst life's challenges. Exploring devotionals together becomes a shared adventure, rich with opportunities for connection and growth.

Interactive Element: Devotional Dialogue Prompts

Create an open dialogue with your partner using these conversation starters:

1. "What are your thoughts on spirituality and how it fits into our lives?"
2. "Is there an experience with devotionals you'd like to share?"
3. "How do you feel about exploring a new way of connecting through devotionals?"

Use these prompts to initiate a conversation, allowing both partners to express their views openly and without judgment. This can be the first step in finding a devotional practice that feels right for both of you.

Reframing Past Devotional Disappointments

We've all had those moments where things don't go as planned, especially in our spiritual practices. Maybe you've sat down with a devotional, hoping it would light a spark, only to feel nothing but a flicker of disappointment. You might have had high expectations, picturing a profound sense of peace and connection, but instead felt inadequate or even like you failed. These experiences can linger, casting a shadow over future attempts. It's essential to face these feelings to acknowledge that unmet expectations are a part of life. It's okay to feel like you didn't quite hit the mark. Recognizing these moments allows you to learn and move forward rather than letting them hold you back.

Reframing these past disappointments can transform them into stepping stones. Instead of seeing them as failures, view them as opportunities for growth. What lessons can you extract from these experiences? Perhaps they taught you about your spiritual needs or highlighted what doesn't work for you. By shifting your focus from failure to growth, you open yourself up to new possibilities. This change in perspective can be incredibly liberating. It allows you to approach devotionals with a fresh mindset, unburdened by the weight of past disappointments. Embrace the idea that each attempt brings you closer to understanding what enriches your spiritual life.

With this newfound perspective, you can explore fresh approaches to your devotional practice. Sometimes, the key lies in trying something new. Experiment with different materials or formats that resonate more deeply with where you are now. Perhaps you haven't yet found the devotional style that speaks to you—whether poetry, art, or even a more interactive format. Setting realistic and achievable goals can also help, allowing you to engage with devotionals in a way that feels rewarding rather than overwhelming. These changes can reignite your interest and commitment, turning what once felt like a chore into a cherished part of your day.

The long-term benefits of reframing these experiences are profound. You may be more open to spiritual exploration and ready to embrace new ideas and practices. This openness can lead to personal growth and a deeper connection with your partner. As you navigate this renewed path together, you'll likely discover insights about yourselves and each other that might have remained hidden. Reframing past experiences enhances your spiritual resilience and strengthens your relational bonds. You're building a foundation that supports both your individual and shared growth, fostering a spiritually rich and fulfilling relationship.

Building Trust in the Process

Have you ever tried sharing something deeply personal only to feel a flicker of doubt about how it might be received? Trust is the bridge that spans this chasm, especially in spiritual practices shared with your partner. It's like laying a foundation of safety and support, where vulnerability isn't just accepted—it's welcomed. When you trust your partner, you're more likely to open up about your spiritual insights and struggles, fostering a deeper connection. This trust encourages you to be brave in your vulnerability, knowing you're met with understanding rather than judgment. This environment allows devotionals to flourish, turning them into a shared experience that strengthens your bond.

Building that trust doesn't happen overnight, but some steps can guide you. One of the most effective ways is through consistency. When both partners are committed to participating regularly in devotional activities, it sends a powerful message of reliability. This consistency creates a rhythm, a dependable pattern that builds trust over time. Alongside this, honest communication is key. Sharing your spiritual experiences, thoughts, and even doubts with one another can nurture an open dialogue. It's about speaking freely and listening intently, ensuring both partners feel valued and heard. This honest exchange becomes a cornerstone of trust, allowing you to navigate spiritual challenges confidently.

Yet, trust can be fragile, sometimes shaken by past betrayals or disappointments. These experiences can linger, casting shadows over your current interactions. The fear of judgment or rejection might make you hesitant to share your innermost thoughts. To overcome these barriers, it helps to acknowledge them openly. Discuss past experiences and how they've impacted your trust. By addressing these issues head-on, you can begin to heal and rebuild. Encourage each other to view the present as a new chapter where trust is actively nurtured, and past wounds are left behind.

Reassurance and patience are your allies, allowing you to move forward with renewed hope.

When trust becomes the foundation of your devotional practice, its impact is profound. You'll likely be more willing to explore and share, diving into spiritual topics with curiosity and openness. This shared exploration can lead to strengthened relational bonds as you engage with one another on a deeper level. The spiritual growth that emerges from this dynamic is individual and collective, enriching your relationship. You may notice a newfound sense of unity and understanding as trust emboldens you to delve into previously intimidating areas. This shared journey of trust and exploration becomes vital to your relationship, enhancing your spiritual and personal connections.

As you cultivate trust, remember it's a living, evolving part of your relationship. Each shared experience and moment of vulnerability and support contribute to a stronger bond. Trust becomes the thread that weaves through your devotionals, creating a tapestry of connection that supports and uplifts both partners. Through this Process, you're building trust in each other and a resilient, compassionate relationship deeply rooted in shared spiritual growth. This foundation will serve you well, allowing you to face future challenges with confidence and grace, knowing that together, you can weather any storm.

CHAPTER 11
52 UNIQUE DAILY REFLECTIONS

Here is a list of 52 daily devotional scriptures, designed to inspire and encourage you throughout the year. Each verse focuses on faith, hope, love, and strength:

1. **Day 1**: *Psalm 118:24* - "This is the day that the Lord has made; let us rejoice and be glad in it."
2. **Day 2**: *Proverbs 3:5-6* - "Trust in the Lord with all your heart and lean not on your own understanding."
3. **Day 3**: *Jeremiah 29:11* - "For I know the plans I have for you, declares the Lord, plans to prosper you and not to harm you."
4. **Day 4**: *Isaiah 41:10* - "Fear not, for I am with you; be not dismayed, for I am your God."
5. **Day 5**: *Matthew 11:28* - "Come to me, all who labor and are heavy laden, and I will give you rest."
6. **Day 6**: *Philippians 4:13* - "I can do all things through Christ who strengthens me."
7. **Day 7**: *Psalm 23:1* - "The Lord is my shepherd; I shall not want."

8. **Day 8**: *Romans 8:28* - "And we know that in all things God works for the good of those who love Him."
9. **Day 9**: *2 Corinthians 5:7* - "For we walk by faith, not by sight."
10. **Day 10**: *1 John 4:19* - "We love because He first loved us."
11. **Day 11**: *Ephesians 2:8-9* - "For by grace you have been saved through faith. And this is not your own doing."
12. **Day 12**: *James 1:2-3* - "Consider it pure joy, my brothers and sisters, whenever you face trials of many kinds."
13. **Day 13**: *Isaiah 40:31* - "But those who hope in the Lord will renew their strength."
14. **Day 14**: *Hebrews 11:1* - "Now faith is the assurance of things hoped for, the conviction of things not seen."
15. **Day 15**: *Colossians 3:23-24* - "Whatever you do, work heartily, as for the Lord and not for men."
16. **Day 16**: *Psalm 46:1* - "God is our refuge and strength, an ever-present help in trouble."
17. **Day 17**: *Matthew 6:33* - "But seek first the kingdom of God and His righteousness."
18. **Day 18**: *John 14:27* - "Peace I leave with you; my peace I give to you."
19. **Day 19**: *Romans 12:2* - "Do not conform to the pattern of this world, but be transformed by the renewing of your mind."
20. **Day 20**: *1 Peter 5:7* - "Cast all your anxiety on Him because He cares for you."
21. **Day 21**: *Galatians 6:9* - "Let us not grow weary of doing good, for in due season we will reap."
22. **Day 22**: *Philippians 4:6-7* - "Do not be anxious about anything, but in everything, by prayer and supplication with thanksgiving."
23. **Day 23**: *2 Timothy 1:7* - "For God gave us a spirit not of fear but of power and love and self-control."
24. **Day 24**: *Psalm 34:8* - "Taste and see that the Lord is good."
25. **Day 25**: *Matthew 5:16* - "Let your light shine before others, that they may see your good deeds."

26. **Day 26**: *Romans 15:13* - "May the God of hope fill you with all joy and peace."
27. **Day 27**: *Micah 6:8* - "What does the Lord require of you but to act justly, love mercy, and walk humbly?"
28. **Day 28**: *John 3:16* - "For God so loved the world that He gave His one and only Son."
29. **Day 29**: *Joshua 1:9* - "Be strong and courageous. Do not be afraid; do not be discouraged."
30. **Day 30**: *1 Thessalonians 5:16-18* - "Rejoice always, pray continually, give thanks in all circumstances."
31. **Day 31**: *Lamentations 3:22-23* - "Because of the Lord's great love we are not consumed."
32. **Day 32**: *Psalm 119:105* - "Your word is a lamp to my feet and a light to my path."
33. **Day 33**: *Proverbs 18:10* - "The name of the Lord is a strong tower."
34. **Day 34**: *1 Corinthians 16:13* - "Be on your guard; stand firm in the faith; be courageous."
35. **Day 35**: *Ephesians 6:10* - "Finally, be strong in the Lord and in His mighty power."
36. **Day 36**: *Psalm 37:4* - "Delight yourself in the Lord, and He will give you the desires of your heart."
37. **Day 37**: *Matthew 7:7* - "Ask, and it will be given to you; seek, and you will find."
38. **Day 38**: *Isaiah 26:3* - "You will keep in perfect peace those whose minds are steadfast."
39. **Day 39**: *John 15:5* - "I am the vine; you are the branches."
40. **Day 40**: *1 Corinthians 13:4-7* - "Love is patient, love is kind."
41. **Day 41**: *Romans 5:8* - "But God demonstrates His own love for us in this: While we were still sinners."
42. **Day 42**: *2 Corinthians 12:9* - "My grace is sufficient for you, for my power is made perfect in weakness."
43. **Day 43**: *Hebrews 13:8* - "Jesus Christ is the same yesterday and today and forever."

44. **Day 44**: *Psalm 55:22* - "Cast your burden on the Lord, and He will sustain you."
45. **Day 45**: *Zephaniah 3:17* - "The Lord your God is in your midst, a mighty one who will save."
46. **Day 46**: *John 10:10* - "I came that they may have life and have it abundantly."
47. **Day 47**: *2 Peter 3:9* - "The Lord is not slow to fulfill His promise."
48. **Day 48**: *Nahum 1:7* - "The Lord is good, a refuge in times of trouble."
49. **Day 49**: *Ecclesiastes 3:1* - "For everything there is a season, and a time for every matter under heaven."
50. **Day 50**: *Revelation 21:4* - "He will wipe every tear from their eyes."
51. **Day 51**: *Psalm 100:4* - "Enter His gates with thanksgiving and His courts with praise."
52. **Day 52**: *1 Chronicles 16:11* - "Seek the Lord and His strength; seek His presence continually."

May these scriptures uplift your spirit and guide your journey.

CHAPTER 12
DAILY REFLECTIONS

Daily Reflections for Growth, Gratitude, and Connection

Week 1: Gratitude

1. Reflect on one thing you're thankful for today.
2. Write down three blessings from this past week.
3. Thank someone who has made a positive impact in your life.
4. Consider how expressing gratitude changes your perspective.
5. Thank God for something you often take for granted.
6. Reflect on the people who bring joy into your life.
7. Spend time appreciating the beauty of God's creation.

Week 2: Love

1. Reflect on how God's love has been evident in your life.

2. Think about someone you can show extra love to today.
3. Meditate on the phrase "love is patient, love is kind" from 1 Corinthians 13.
4. Consider how forgiveness is an act of love.
5. Reflect on ways to love yourself as God loves you.
6. Pray for someone who is struggling and needs love.
7. Think of a time when love helped you overcome a challenge.

Week 3: Peace

1. Reflect on a moment when you felt true peace.
2. Pray for peace in a specific area of your life.
3. Consider how forgiveness can bring peace to your heart.
4. Meditate on the words "Be still and know that I am God" (Psalm 46:10).
5. Think about how trusting God can calm your worries.
6. Pray for peace in a relationship that feels strained.
7. Reflect on how Jesus is the "Prince of Peace" in your life.

Week 4: Faith

1. Recall a time when your faith was tested but strengthened.
2. Reflect on a Bible verse that reminds you to trust in God.
3. Consider how small acts of faith can grow into great changes.
4. Pray for faith to face an uncertain situation.
5. Reflect on what "walking by faith, not by sight" means to you.
6. Thank God for His faithfulness in your life.

7. Think about someone whose faith inspires you and pray for them.

Week 5: Joy

1. Reflect on something that brought you joy recently.
2. Thank God for the gift of laughter.
3. Consider how serving others brings lasting joy.
4. Meditate on the words "The joy of the Lord is my strength" (Nehemiah 8:10).
5. Reflect on how gratitude contributes to your joy.
6. Pray for someone who could use a little more joy in their life.
7. Think about how God's presence fills your heart with joy.

Week 6: Strength

1. Reflect on a time when God gave you strength in a challenge.
2. Pray for strength in an area where you feel weak.
3. Meditate on Philippians 4:13: "I can do all things through Christ who strengthens me."
4. Think of someone who is struggling and pray for their strength.
5. Reflect on how rest can renew your physical and spiritual strength.
6. Thank God for the strength He provides every day.
7. Consider how challenges shape your character and build resilience.

Week 7: Kindness

1. Reflect on an act of kindness you received recently.
2. Think about how you can show kindness to someone today.
3. Consider how kindness reflects God's love for others.
4. Pray for a heart that looks for opportunities to serve others.
5. Meditate on Ephesians 4:32: "Be kind and compassionate to one another."
6. Reflect on how kindness can heal relationships.
7. Think of a small act of kindness that can brighten someone's day.

Week 8: Hope

1. Reflect on what brings you hope in difficult times.
2. Pray for someone who may feel hopeless or discouraged.
3. Meditate on Jeremiah 29:11: "For I know the plans I have for you, declares the Lord."
4. Consider how hope in God differs from worldly hope.
5. Thank God for His promises that give you hope.
6. Reflect on how sharing hope with others encourages your spirit.
7. Think about a time when hope was restored in your life.

Week 9: Forgiveness

1. Reflect on how forgiving others sets you free.
2. Pray for someone who has hurt you and release your bitterness.

3. Meditate on Colossians 3:13: "Forgive as the Lord forgave you."
4. Consider how forgiveness brings healing to your soul.

This structure can be used daily or adjusted as needed, providing a meaningful and balanced journey over 60 days.

The daily reflections outlined above can be highly beneficial for couples because they focus on themes that nurture personal growth, mutual understanding, and a stronger spiritual foundation. Here's how these reflections positively impact relationships:

1. Encouraging Gratitude (Week 1)

- **Why it helps couples**: Practicing gratitude shifts the focus from complaints to blessings, fostering appreciation for one another. Recognizing the good in each other strengthens emotional bonds and reduces resentment.
- **Practical outcome**: Couples may become more intentional in expressing thanks for small acts of kindness, deepening their connection.

2. Building Love (Week 2)

- **Why it helps couples**: Love is central to any relationship, and reflecting on how to express and receive love can help couples grow closer. By meditating on love, couples learn to prioritize selflessness, patience, and understanding.
- **Practical outcome**: Acts of love become more deliberate,

and couples can focus on areas such as forgiveness and effective communication.

3. Cultivating Peace (Week 3)

- **Why it helps couples**: Reflecting on peace helps couples manage conflict, anxiety, and external pressures. It emphasizes the importance of creating a tranquil and supportive environment in their relationship.
- **Practical outcome**: Partners can work toward peaceful resolution of conflicts and nurture a home environment filled with calm and harmony.

4. Strengthening Faith (Week 4)

- **Why it helps couples**: Faith provides a solid foundation for navigating challenges together. Reflecting on faith helps couples trust in God's plan for their relationship and depend on Him during difficult seasons.
- **Practical outcome**: Couples may learn to pray together, support each other's spiritual growth, and view obstacles as opportunities for growth.

5. Embracing Joy (Week 5)

- **Why it helps couples**: Joy is an essential part of a thriving relationship. Reflecting on joy encourages couples to celebrate the good times and find positivity even in challenging moments.

- **Practical outcome**: Partners may seek shared experiences that bring joy, such as quality time, laughter, and pursuing shared hobbies.

6. Drawing Strength (Week 6)

- **Why it helps couples**: Life's challenges can test a relationship. Reflecting on strength reminds couples that they can rely on God and each other for support.
- **Practical outcome**: Partners become more resilient together, finding comfort in their shared faith and mutual encouragement during tough times.

7. Practicing Kindness (Week 7)

- **Why it helps couples**: Kindness is a key ingredient in building trust and maintaining a positive dynamic. Reflecting on kindness helps couples identify ways to serve and uplift one another.
- **Practical outcome**: Couples can intentionally practice small, meaningful acts of kindness that reinforce their love and care.

8. Finding Hope (Week 8)

- **Why it helps couples**: Hope provides the motivation to keep moving forward, even in seasons of difficulty. Reflecting on hope helps couples focus on their shared future and the promises of God.

- **Practical outcome**: Partners may feel more united in overcoming setbacks and pursuing their dreams together.

9. Embracing Forgiveness (Week 9)

- **Why it helps couples**: No relationship is without mistakes. Reflecting on forgiveness fosters empathy, humility, and healing, enabling couples to move forward from hurt.
- **Practical outcome**: Forgiveness creates emotional freedom and strengthens trust, preventing unresolved issues from festering.

Overall Benefits for Couples

1. **Improved Communication**: Discussing reflections together can encourage open, meaningful conversations about faith, feelings, and goals.
2. **Strengthened Spiritual Bond**: Sharing a daily practice of reflection and prayer reinforces the spiritual foundation of the relationship.
3. **Conflict Resolution**: Many themes (peace, kindness, forgiveness) provide tools for navigating disagreements.
4. **Greater Intimacy**: Reflecting on love, gratitude, and joy nurtures emotional and spiritual closeness.
5. **Renewed Perspective**: Daily focus on positive themes shifts attention from problems to opportunities for growth and unity.

By committing to these reflections, couples not only grow individually but also build a relationship rooted in love, faith, and mutual understanding.

CHAPTER 13

THE TRANSFORMATIVE POWER OF DAILY REFLECTIONS AND DEVOTIONS

Why Daily Devotions and Reflections Are Vital to Spiritual Growth

Daily reflections and devotions are transformative practices that serve as a foundation for spiritual growth, personal transformation, and a closer relationship with God. These practices involve intentionally dedicating time daily to focus on spiritual truths, meditating on scripture, and evaluating one's thoughts and actions in light of faith and values. Daily devotions and reflections act as an anchor in a fast-paced world filled with distractions, helping individuals remain grounded and aligned with their purpose and divine calling.

Devotions are more than a routine—they are a sacred time for communion with God. Whether reading scripture, praying, or journaling, devotions open the door to divine inspiration, clarity, and strength. This time allows believers to immerse themselves in the Word of God, drawing wisdom and guidance for navigating life's challenges. During these moments, individuals often experience spiritual renewal, a sense of peace, and the assurance that they are not alone on their journey.

Reflections complement devotions by encouraging introspection and self-awareness. In a reflective state, individuals assess their thoughts, decisions, and behaviors, allowing them to identify growth areas and moments of gratitude. Reflection invites believers to confront their struggles, celebrate progress, and realign with God's purpose. It cultivates humility, fostering an open heart ready for guidance and correction. These practices also create space for acknowledging and releasing fears, doubts, and burdens, replacing them with faith, trust, and hope.

The significance of daily devotions and reflections extends beyond the individual. By consistently engaging in these practices, believers strengthen their spiritual foundation, which impacts their relationships and interactions with others. A spiritually grounded person exudes compassion, patience, and understanding, fostering meaningful connections with family, friends, and the broader community. These practices empower individuals to live out their faith authentically, providing encouragement and light to those around them.

Daily devotions and reflections also enhance emotional and mental well-being. Pausing, praying, and pondering create balance, reducing stress and anxiety. By turning to scripture and spiritual truths, individuals find comfort and strength, equipping them to face life's uncertainties with courage and resilience. Over time, these practices help to develop a mindset that focuses on gratitude, hope, and trust, fostering a more positive outlook on life.

This chapter explores the profound benefits of daily reflections and devotions under several key subtopics. These include their role in fostering a deeper relationship with God, enhancing emotional and mental well-being, building resilience in the face of challenges, and cultivating virtues such as patience, forgiveness, and humility. Additionally, we will examine how these practices can serve as a source of strength in times of adversity, providing a path to healing and restoration.

Whether you are seeking to deepen your spiritual walk, find clarity in your daily life, or strengthen your relationships, daily devotions and reflections offer a transformative path. They are rituals and opportunities to encounter God's presence, draw wisdom from His Word, and grow into who He has called you to be.

Enhancing Spiritual Growth

Deepening Faith

Daily reflections and devotions allow individuals to engage with Scripture, reinforcing their trust in God. By meditating on His Word, believers gain insights into His promises and character. This process strengthens faith, enabling them to navigate challenges with confidence and hope.

Building a Personal Relationship with God

Consistent devotion is vital in nurturing a personal and intimate relationship with God. Just as strong relationships in daily life require time, communication, and intentionality, so does a relationship with the Creator. Through regular practices like prayer, meditation, and time in scripture, individuals can develop a deeper understanding of God's character, His will, and His promises, creating opportunities for moments of profound connection.

Experiencing God Through Prayer

Prayer is the cornerstone of this relationship, serving as conversation and communion with God. It allows individuals to share their hearts openly—bringing their joys, fears, struggles and hopes before Him. For example, a person facing a challenging decision may pray for wisdom, and through that act of surrender, they might feel God's gentle reassurance, guiding them toward the best path. This consistent communication builds trust and familiarity, fostering a sense of closeness to God.

In addition to speaking, listening during prayer is equally important. By creating moments of silence, individuals can attune their hearts to God's still, small voice. For example, after praying for clarity about a difficult situation, someone might sense a newfound peace or receive unexpected insights during their quiet moments—confirming that God is actively working in their life.

Meditation on God's Word

Meditation on scripture is another powerful way to deepen intimacy with God. Through careful study and reflection on biblical passages, individuals can uncover timeless truths about God's love, mercy, and faithfulness. For instance, reflecting on Psalm 23 ("The Lord is my shepherd...") can remind someone feeling lost that God is their constant guide and protector. By internalizing such truths, individuals draw closer to God and learn to trust Him more fully in every aspect of life.

Meditating on God's Word helps individuals align their lives with His will. As they ponder passages that speak to obedience, forgiveness, or love, they begin to see how these principles can be applied to their relationships and decisions. Over time, this intentional focus transforms their understanding of God and their character and actions.

Intimacy Through Worship

Worship is another avenue for building a relationship with God. Whether through singing, journaling or simply expressing gratitude, worship shifts the focus away from life's challenges and onto God's greatness. For example, someone who feels weighed down by stress might choose to worship by singing songs of praise, redirecting their heart toward God's power and faithfulness. In doing so, they experience a more profound sense of peace and connection as worship becomes a gateway to His presence.

Fostering Peace and Reassurance

A personal relationship with God fosters peace, guidance, and reassurance. In times of uncertainty, individuals can rest in knowing that God is sovereign and faithful. For instance, someone overwhelmed by financial struggles might turn to Philippians 4:6-7 ("Do not be anxious about anything...") during their devotional time, finding comfort in the promise of God's peace that surpasses understanding.

This relationship also provides a steady source of guidance. As believers seek God's will through prayer and scripture, they learn to discern His direction for their lives. For example, someone considering a career change might sense God's leading through prayer, scripture study, and the counsel of trusted mentors. This guidance, rooted in an intimate connection with God, brings confidence and clarity even in complex situations.

Reassurance in God's Presence

Perhaps the most profound aspect of a personal relationship with God is the reassurance of His constant presence. Through consistent devotion, individuals experience a tangible awareness of God walking alongside them, even in their darkest moments. This awareness brings strength as they remember that they are never alone. For example, someone enduring grief might feel God's comforting presence during prayer, reminding them of His promise to be near the brokenhearted (Psalm 34:18).

The Transformational Impact

As individuals cultivate their relationship with God through consistent devotion, their lives are transformed. They begin to see the world through His eyes, respond to challenges with faith rather than fear, and interact with others in ways that reflect His love and grace. This transformation is not limited to personal growth—it also influences families, communities, and workplaces as God's presence flows through their lives to bless others.

Encouraging Consistency in Worship

Daily devotions cultivate a habit of worship that keeps faith at the forefront of one's life. Regular engagement with God's Word prevents spiritual stagnation, helping believers stay connected to their Creator even during busy or challenging seasons.

Promoting Emotional Well-Being

Reducing Stress and Anxiety

Taking time for reflection provides a sense of calm and clarity. Devotions often involve moments of silence, prayer, or journaling, which help individuals process emotions and surrender worries to God. This practice reduces stress and promotes a sense of inner peace.

Fostering Gratitude

Reflecting on daily blessings shifts focus from what is lacking to what is present. Gratitude transforms perspectives, enabling individuals to find joy in small things and approach life with a more positive attitude.

Boosting Emotional Resilience

Through reflection and devotions, individuals can confront challenges with a renewed perspective. By grounding themselves in faith and hope, they build emotional resilience to face life's uncertainties and setbacks with grace.

Enhancing Personal Growth

Promoting Self-Awareness

Daily reflections encourage individuals to examine their thoughts, actions, and motivations. This introspection fosters self-awareness, helping people recognize areas for improvement and celebrate personal victories.

Encouraging Goal-Setting

Regular reflection offers a chance to evaluate personal and spiritual goals. It allows individuals to align their daily actions with their values and aspirations, creating a more purposeful life.

Strengthening Character

Devotional practices instill virtues such as patience, kindness, humility, and forgiveness. These qualities shape a person's character, enabling them to interact with others in ways that reflect their faith and values.

Building Stronger Relationships

Fostering Communication

For couples or families, shared reflections and devotions provide opportunities to connect on a deeper level. Discussing themes like gratitude, love, and forgiveness encourages open and honest communication.

Cultivating Compassion

Daily devotions often include prayers for others, which nurture empathy and compassion. Reflecting on how to serve and support loved ones fosters stronger and more meaningful relationships.

Resolving Conflicts

Themes of forgiveness, peace, and kindness help individuals approach conflicts with humility and understanding. Reflection provides the tools to navigate disagreements constructively, strengthening bonds over time.

. . .

Aligning Life with Purpose

Finding Clarity and Direction

Reflection helps individuals discern God's purpose for their lives. Meditating on Scripture and seeking divine guidance provides clarity in decision-making and aligns daily actions with long-term goals.

Living Intentionally

By focusing on what truly matters, daily devotions encourage intentional living. This practice helps individuals prioritize spiritual growth, relationships, and meaningful contributions over distractions.

Rekindling Passion and Hope

Daily engagement with Scripture reignites passion for one's faith and hope for the future. This renewed perspective inspires individuals to persevere in their spiritual journey and trust in God's plan.

Fostering a Positive Mindset

Shifting Perspective

Daily reflections remind individuals of God's sovereignty and the eternal perspective of life. This mindset helps believers view temporary struggles in light of God's greater plan, bringing peace and optimism.

Replacing Negative Thoughts with Truth

Scripture-based reflections combat negative thinking by replacing lies with God's truth. By focusing on uplifting and affirming messages, individuals can transform their mindset and cultivate joy.

Inspiring Daily Gratitude

Devotions that focus on thankfulness encourage individuals to find blessings in every moment. A consistent gratitude practice nurtures contentment and reduces tendencies toward comparison or dissatisfaction.

Strengthening Faith During Difficult Seasons

Offering Comfort in Trials

Daily devotions provide solace during life's most challenging moments. By meditating on God's promises, individuals find comfort in His faithfulness and presence, even in times of sorrow or uncertainty.

Restoring Hope

Devotions focused on hope remind believers of God's redemptive power. These reflections inspire perseverance, helping individuals remain steadfast in their faith despite hardships.   .

Encouraging Patience

Reflection on Scriptures about waiting and trusting in God's timing cultivates patience. This practice teaches individuals to endure trials with grace, trusting that God is working for their good.

Encouraging Community and Connection

Fostering Shared Spiritual Practices

Engaging in devotions as a group, whether with family, friends, or a small community, strengthens bonds and builds spiritual accountability. Shared reflections encourage unity and mutual support.

Inspiring Service to Others

Devotions that focus on serving others motivate individuals to extend compassion and generosity to their communities. Reflecting on Jesus' example inspires acts of kindness and selflessness.

Celebrating Faith Together

Participating in shared devotions creates opportunities for collective worship and thanksgiving. This communal practice deepens relationships and reinforces shared values.

Nurturing Long-Term Spiritual Habits

Developing Discipline

Consistent devotions cultivate a discipline that extends into other areas of life. This habit strengthens focus, time management, and commitment to personal growth.

Encouraging Lifelong Learning

Daily engagement with Scripture promotes continual learning and discovery of God's Word. This lifelong journey enriches faith and deepens understanding of spiritual truths.

Building a Legacy of Faith

Modeling daily reflections for children or loved ones sets a powerful example of faith in action. This practice creates a spiritual legacy that impacts future generations.

· · ·

Practical Tips for Starting Daily Reflections and Devotions

Set a Regular Time

Choose a specific time each day for devotions, whether in the morning, during lunch, or before bed. Consistency helps establish the habit.

Create a Sacred Space

Designate a quiet, comfortable space for reflections, free from distractions. This helps create an environment conducive to focus and peace.

Use Resources

Utilize devotional books, apps, or journals to guide your practice. These resources offer structured content and themes to inspire deeper engagement.

Start Small

Begin with a few minutes a day and gradually increase the time as the habit becomes more ingrained. The key is consistency, not duration.

Incorporate Prayer and Journaling

Pair reflections with prayer and journaling to personalize the experience. Writing down thoughts and prayers helps process emotions and track spiritual growth.

Daily reflections and devotions are transformative practices that nurture the mind, heart, and soul. They provide clarity, purpose, and peace while strengthening relationships and fostering resilience. By dedicating time to engage with Scripture, prayer, and introspection, individuals can experience profound personal and spiritual growth.

Whether practiced alone or with others, daily devotions serve as a powerful tool for aligning life with God's will, cultivating gratitude, and living intentionally. The benefits are far-reaching, offering joy, hope, and strength to navigate the journey of life with faith and purpose.

REVIEW

Strengthening Bonds Together

Now that you've explored *Relationship Devotional for Couples* and discovered ways to deepen your connection, it's time to share your experience with others who are searching for the same guidance.

By leaving your honest opinion of this book on Amazon, you'll help other couples find the encouragement they need to grow closer to each other and to God. Your words can show them that hope and love are always within reach.

Thank you for your help. The beauty of love and faith is kept alive when we share our stories—and you're helping us do just that.

Click here to leave your review on Amazon.

With gratitude,

Dean Ramsey

CONCLUSION

As you reach the end of this journey, take a moment to reflect on the path you've traveled through these pages. We've delved into the heart of nurturing a strong, resilient relationship, exploring how daily devotionals, communication, faith, intimacy, and resilience can transform your connection. Together, we've unpacked these elements' profound impact on building a relationship that survives and thrives.

The vision of this book has always been clear: to offer you unique, non-repetitive content that integrates proven strategies and meaningful Bible verses. The aim has been to help you and your partner deepen your connection with each other and on your spiritual journey. It's been about creating a roadmap that guides you through life's challenges, providing the tools to rekindle love, enhance communication, and build faith.

Throughout each chapter, we've shared key insights and practical strategies. From establishing a spiritual core to integrating diverse beliefs, you've learned how to create a sacred space for devotion and map your faith journey together. We've explored the art of mindful listening, the balance of busy schedules, and the power of prayer. By embracing these practices, you've been equipped to navigate life's transitions and celebrations, ensuring that your relationship remains strong and vibrant.

I want to speak directly to you. Your commitment to improving your relationship through these practices is genuinely commendable. You've shown a willingness to grow, challenge, and nurture what is most precious. This journey isn't always easy, but your dedication to each other speaks volumes. You are not alone on this path, and your efforts are seen and valued.

I encourage you to embrace these daily devotional practices and strategies as you progress. Transformation and deeper connection are within your reach, even amidst the busiest days. These moments of reflection, prayer, and communication can be your anchors, grounding you when life feels overwhelming. Remember, the small, consistent steps lead to meaningful change.

Now, it's time for action. Set specific goals for implementing the insights you've gained. Whether it's dedicating time to daily devotionals, improving your communication, or nurturing your spiritual and emotional bonds, take these steps with purpose. Your relationship is a living, evolving entity, and these actions will help it grow stronger.

Thank you for embarking on this journey with me. Your dedication to strengthening your relationship and faith is inspiring. It's been an honor to walk alongside you and offer guidance and support through these pages.

As you look to the future, remember that your journey doesn't end here. Continue evolving and growing together, embracing the ongoing nature of your spiritual and relational path. Be open to new experiences, and let each moment deepen your understanding and connection. Your relationship is a testament to love, resilience, and faith. Keep nurturing it, and it will continue to flourish.

May your days ahead be filled with love, joy, and a deeper connection to each other and your shared spiritual journey. Here's to the beautiful future you are creating together.

BIBLIOGRAPHY

Aligned Hope. (n.d.). *Mobile apps to strengthen your marriage (try them out on your phone)*. Retrieved from https://alignedhope.com/mobile-apps-to-strengthen-your-marriage-try-them-out-on-your-phone/

Biblestudytools.com. (n.d.). *25+ Bible verses about relationships: Best scripture quotes*. Retrieved from https://www.biblestudytools.com/topical-verses/relationship-bible-verses/

Biblestudytools.com. (n.d.). *12 hopeful Bible verses for times of transition*. Retrieved from https://www.biblestudytools.com/bible-study/topical-studies/12-hopeful-bible-verses-for-times-of-transition.html

Catholic Company. (n.d.). *How to make an at-home prayer corner*. Retrieved from https://www.catholiccompany.com/magazine/your-home-prayer-corner-6679/

Crosswalk.com. (n.d.). *Clothe others with dignity and strength - Crosswalk couples*. Retrieved from https://www.crosswalk.com/devotionals/crosswalk-couples-devotional/

Credello.com. (n.d.). *Experts explain how to navigate financial stress in relationships*. Retrieved from https://www.credello.com/financial-resources/trending/navigating-financial-stress-in-relationships/

Eagle Family Ministries. (n.d.). *Stewarding finances as a Christian couple*. Retrieved from https://www.eaglefamily.org/stewarding-finances-as-a-christian-couple/

FamilyLife. (n.d.). *What will be your legacy?* Retrieved from https://www.familylife.com/articles/topics/marriage/staying-married/husbands/what-will-be-your-legacy/

Forbes.com. (2019, October 24). *Your marriage or your job? How to balance your career and your relationship*. Retrieved from https://www.forbes.com/sites/erikaboissiere/2019/10/24/your-marriage-or-your-job-how-to-balance-your-career-and-your-relationship/

Focus on the Family Canada. (n.d.). *How to strengthen your spiritual connection in marriage*. Retrieved from https://www.focusonthefamily.ca/content/how-to-strengthen-your-spiritual-connection-in-marriage

Gottman Connect. (n.d.). *Gottman relationship checkup (for couples)*. Retrieved from https://gottmanconnect.com/checkup/couples

Grey Journal. (n.d.). *Communication strategies for busy couples*. Retrieved from https://greyjournal.net/play/dating/communication-strategies-for-busy-couples/

Holding Hope MFT. (n.d.). *Active listening in relationships: A path to deeper intimacy*. Retrieved from https://holdinghopemft.com/active-listening-a-key-to-deeper-intimacy-and-understanding-in-your-relationship/

Holding Hope MFT. (n.d.). *Goal setting in relationships: A therapist's guide for couples.* Retrieved from https://holdinghopemft.com/the-power-of-goal-setting-in-relationships-a-step-by-step-guide-for-couples/

Investopedia.com. (2015, December 3). *How to create a budget with your spouse (in 7 steps).* Retrieved from https://www.investopedia.com/articles/personal-finance/120315/how-create-budget-your-spouse.asp

Ibelieve.com. (n.d.). *Strengthening your marriage through shared spiritual practices.* Retrieved from https://www.ibelieve.com/relation-ships/strengthening-your-marriage-through-shared-spiritual-practices.html

Institute for Family Studies. (n.d.). *When religious couples pray.* Retrieved from https://ifstudies.org/blog/when-religious-couples-pray#:~:text=Prayer%20has%20also%20been%20associated%20with%20im-proved%20conflict%20resolution

Kveller.com. (n.d.). *Cokie Roberts showed us what a modern interfaith marriage can look like.* Retrieved from https://www.kveller.com/cokie-roberts-showed-us-what-a-modern-interfaith-marriage-can-look-like/

Marriage.com. (n.d.). *30 couple bonding activities to strengthen the relationship.* Retrieved from https://www.marriage.com/advice/relationship/couple-bonding-activities-to-strengthen-the-relationship/

Marriage.com. (n.d.). *10 techniques for couples to align relationships and time.* Retrieved from https://www.marriage.com/advice/relationship/time-management-techniques-for-couples/

Medium.com. (n.d.). *The role of faith in Christian couples counseling: A path to healing.* Retrieved from https://medium.com/@james-william/the-role-of-faith-in-christian-couples-counseling-a-path-to-healing-5cb3af53f944

Metro Family Magazine. (n.d.). *Creating a harmonious holiday: Tips & advice for interfaith families.* Retrieved from https://www.metrofamilymagazine.com/creating-a-harmonious-holiday-tips-advice-for-interfaith-families/

Open Bible. (n.d.). *24 Bible verses about marriage and finances.* Retrieved from https://www.openbible.info/topics/marriage_and_finances

Psychology Today. (2021, March). *Does personal growth benefit a relationship?* Retrieved from https://www.psychologytoday.com/us/blog/talking-apes/202103/does-personal-growth-benefit-a-relationship

Retirement.berkeley.edu. (n.d.). *Retirement and your relationship.* Retrieved from https://retirement.berkeley.edu/retirement-planning/retirement-and-your-relationship

Serenity in Suffering. (n.d.). *Creating a sacred space.* Retrieved from https://serenityinsuffering.com/creating-a-sacred-space/

Soulessencepsychotherapy.com. (n.d.). *5 spiritual morning routine ideas to incorporate into your day.* Retrieved from https://www.soulessencepsychotherapy.com/post/spiritual-routine

Sparkle and Shine Today. (n.d.). *8 feng shui tips to help you feel at peace in your home.* Retrieved from https://www.sparkleandshine.today/blog/feng-shui-tips-to-feel-at-peace/

Transitions Counseling Inc. (n.d.). *Celebrating milestones and successes together.* Retrieved from https://transitionscounselinginc.com/celebrating-milestones-and-successes-together-a-norfork-ma-therapist-discusses/#:~:text=These%20milestones%2C%20whether%20they%20mark

WordPress.com. (2009, December 1). *Interfaith marriage: A love story | Being both.* Retrieved from https://onbeingboth.wordpress.com/2009/12/01/interfaith-marriage-a-love-story/

Made in the USA
Middletown, DE
28 May 2025

76165787R00090